EXPLORING
Central Alberta's
PARKLAND

A Guide to Red Deer's Waskasoo Park & Beyond
by Anna Robertson

Illustrations by Gary Ross

Foreword by Dr. Charles Bird

Rocky
Mountain Books

Photo Credits
The City of Red Deer, Waskasoo Park Collection; the Kerry Wood Nature Centre, and the David Thompson Country Tourist Council.
Marlene Walentowitz: page 14; Rich White: page 40; Jane Ross: page 133; Gillean Daffern: pages 136 and 137.
All historical photographs courtesy of the Red Deer and District Archives except for pages 41, 52, 53, 70 and 75, which are courtesy of the Glenbow Archives.
All illustrations by Gary Ross except for Gary Van Overloop page 18.
Maps provided by the City of Red Deer.

Published by
Rocky Mountain Books
#4 Spruce Centre SW
RMB **Calgary, Alberta T3C 3B3**

The publisher gratefully acknowledges the assistance provided by the Alberta Foundation for the Arts and by the federal Department of Canadian Heritage.

COMMITTED TO THE DEVELOPMENT OF CULTURE AND THE ARTS

Canadian Cataloguing in Publication Data

Robertson, Anna, 1961-
    Exploring Central Alberta's parkland

    Includes bibliographical references and index.
    ISBN 0-921102-49-6

    1. Waskasoo Park (Alta.)--Guidebooks. 2. Alberta--Guidebooks. I. Ross, Gary, 1961- II. Title.
FC3699.W43Z55 1996   917.123'3043   C96-910335-2
F1079.5.R43R62 1996

Contents

Foreword

Waskasoo Park and areas in and near the Red Deer River drainage basin are of considerable interest from a natural history point of view as here we have a very rich assembly of species due to the mixing of many different floristic and faunistic elements. Prairie species occur on south-facing hillsides: areas of aspen parkland have their characteristic aspen grove and intervening grassland species; mountain and boreal species enter the area, especially on north-facing slopes in river and ravine situations; there are also small areas of boreal black spruce and tamarack towards the mountains. In addition, extensive agricultural and urban developments have resulted in the introduction of various crop and garden plants as well as numerous weedy species.

The Red Deer River valley is an area of great scenic beauty and is of great value from a recreational point of view. Agriculture has left it largely untouched as the rough topography and varied soil types are not amenable to cultivation. Visitors see the valley much as it was before white men settled the area. Relatively untouched "wilderness" areas of this sort have long been sought out for their "peace and quiet" and they act as focal points for rest and recreation.

The Red Deer River valley is also of great importance as being a corridor where its varied topography allows mountain and boreal species to occur on north-facing slopes far to the east of their normal distribution, and prairie and badland species on south-facing slopes to extend far to the northwest of their ordinary range. The steep slopes themselves have assured protection for numerous seldom encountered species. The belt of relatively undisturbed vegetation along the river has also allowed bird, mammal and other faunistic species to not only live in the valley, but also occur farther east or west than would otherwise be the case.

The Red Deer River area was one of interest to early naturalists such as the birder P. A. Taverner and the botanist John Macoun. The Red Deer River Naturalists, centred in Red Deer, started in 1906 as a chapter of the Alberta Natural History Club. This group has continued to be active over the years and has done much to point out and conserve the natural environment of the area. The Kerry Wood Nature Centre in Red Deer has become a world centre for natural history study. The City of Red Deer had the foresight to preserve numerous valley and ravine areas in their natural conditions and to provide access to them by means of trail systems. Red Deer has thus become one of the most attractive cities in Canada. The Red Deer Museum and Archives has an excellent collection of artifacts and documents pertaining to the history of the area. The

Buffalo Lake Naturalists Club, centred in Stettler, got underway in 1973. It has done much to point out the uniqueness and value of the Red Deer River drainage basin east of the City of Red Deer.

The major recommendation of a recent study of the Red Deer River corridor was that development should be such that the area be left as much as possible as it is. The area is being managed quite well at the present time. Management change would likely result in a deterioration of the pristine nature of the region. Input came from numerous groups and individuals and it is encouraging that there is such widespread feeling for the protection of the region.

This publication provides a fascinating look at Waskasoo Park and nearby areas. It sums up the work of many keen local individuals and will be of interest to a wide range of people. Its historical, ecological, natural history observations and style of writing provide intimate detail seldom found in books dealing with other areas.

Dr. Charles D. Bird

This book was made possible with the funding assistance of:
- Red Deer Community Futures Committee
- Red Deer Community Foundation
- Red Deer Heritage Foundation
- City of Red Deer
- Red Deer River Naturalists
- Federation of Alberta Naturalists

Introduction

Because of the incredible bio-diversity of the Western Canadian parklands, Central Alberta has long been an active centre for the naturalist movement. Even in the earliest years of settlement, there was a deep and widespread appreciation of the native flora and fauna, thereby prompting a number of organized efforts both to study and to preserve these ecological wonders.

The first naturalist organization was the North-West Entomological Society, which was formed at Blackfalds, Alberta in March 1899. This group was succeeded in 1902 by a broader association, the Territorial Natural History Society.

These pioneer naturalists placed a strong emphasis on education. A number of field clubs were organized in local schools. Prizes were offered for children's exhibits at local fairs. As well, small natural history museums were established at Blackfalds, Calgary and Regina.

Following the creation of the provinces of Alberta and Saskatchewan in 1905, the Alberta Natural History Society was formed at the Town of Innisfail in the spring of 1906. Within a few months, a branch of the society was established in Red Deer. Additional branches were later formed at Erskine, Stettler and Medicine Hat. The Edmonton Natural History Club became an affiliate in 1910.

The ANHS encouraged its members to produce scientific papers and check lists on a variety of subjects. An ambitious program was launched with three booklets eventually being printed. In the early 1920s, the society successfully lobbied to have a beautiful 230-acre natural area, owned by local homesteader John Jost Gaetz on the east side of the City of Red Deer, designated as a Dominion Bird Sanctuary.

Over the next three decades, as the pace of new settlement slackened and many of the pioneer naturalists passed on, the ANHS gradually dwindled in size. By the time of the Second World War, only the Red Deer branch remained active. Nevertheless, its members continued to work on a number of conservation, advocacy and educational projects.

The Red Deer group, with the leadership of local author and naturalist Kerry Wood, was particularly dedicated to fending off threats to the Gaetz Lakes Sanctuary. These challenges included destructive intrusions from an adjacent military training camp and, later, the near destruction of the wooded areas by a fire set by a careless City of Red Deer work crew. There were also numerous ill-conceived proposals by government officials such as logging the escarpment areas, using the oxbow lake as a sewage pond and turning the sanctuary into an amusement park. In 1970-71, there was extensive damage to the second Gaetz Lake due to a poorly installed storm sewer from the Deerhome Institution.

The Alberta Natural History Society experienced a strong resurgence during the 1970s. There was a growing public awareness of environmental problems and concerns. The group, which was renamed the Red Deer River Naturalists in 1976 to avoid confusion with the new Federation of Alberta Naturalists, became even more active as it tackled such controversial environmental issues as the construction of the Dickson Dam, developments in the national parks, and new policies and proposals for the eastern slopes.

In the early 1980s, when the new Waskasoo Park was being developed in the City of Red Deer, the Red Deer River Naturalists energetically lobbied the planners and decision makers to ensure the preservation, not only of the Gaetz Lakes Sanctuary, but also the other natural areas along the river valley. One of the most effective strategies used was simply to take the park planners on outings so that they could see the richness and beauty of these natural areas for themselves.

The RDRN advocated an "onion-skin" approach with the inner-core of ecologically sensitive areas being highly protected, the outer-core becoming partially protected, and buffer zones being created next to the developed areas. Great emphasis was also placed on the need to maintain continuous, natural wildlife corridors throughout the proposed park.

The results have been impressive. The City of Red Deer has been able, not only to create a park full of such recreational opportunities as a first-rate trail system, three interpretive centres and many sports facilities, but also to retain many of the irreplaceable natural features of the river valley. As such, Waskasoo Park has become more than a popular public attraction. It is also a vital community asset that is truly outstanding in the Province of Alberta.

This book is a key to discovering these wonderful attractions and beautiful natural features. In keeping with the long-standing efforts of the local naturalist organizations, this publication strives to make readers aware of the natural heritage around them and to further the cause of environmental preservation through that awareness. Hopefully, as a consequence, the discoveries in the parkland will provide much enjoyment to both present and future generations.

Michael Dawe
November 1995

The Land Through Time

Sub–tropical Red Deer

Imagine Central Alberta 60 million years ago. The earth's crust has buckled and heaved into young Rocky Mountains to the west. The salt water of the Bearspaw Sea, once blanketing most of North America, has withdrawn to the north and east to mingle with the ancestral Arctic and Atlantic oceans. The old sea bottom has risen as well, exposing its sediments to the hot sun. Mighty rivers course down the steep mountain slopes, tearing at the rock and carrying their booty eastward to the plains. As these rivers reach Red Deer, their headlong rush is arrested in lush deltas, swamps and lakes. The silt and sand transported from the mountains is laid to rest below the warm waters.

A shallow backswamp lies still, its stagnant waters barren of fish. Huge dragonflies zip over its surface, scooping their insect prey out of the air. Beetles and beetle larvae navigate the tea–coloured waters in a perpetual search for food. Snails hide among the leaves of water lilies or burrow in the soft muck.

Nearby, a cow–like pantodont shuffles among the horsetails and willows, stopping occasionally to dig in the rich dirt with its snout. It bites at some roots and then moves on. A crash in the forest sends it running for cover.

A large bird takes off from the crown of a dawn redwood and glides over the forested valley. It scans the countryside, turns, then heads south to a favourite feeding area. A small lake ringed with primitive birch trees has swelled during the spring runoff, spilled over its banks and flooded some old stream channels. Now the water level has dropped and a school of smelt are trapped in one of the channels. Many will die and become buried in the muck; others will make a tasty meal for a hungry bird. Grabbing a beakful, the bird flaps heavily to the top of a large–leafed tree. Below, an alligator–like *Champsosaurus* silently slides into the lake, mouth agape, to catch a few fish of its own.

A time traveller would hardly recognize this semi–tropical environment as Central Alberta. Although most of these plants and animals are extinct, many of their relatives still thrive in places such as China, Japan and the southeastern United States.

The Fossil Record

Our knowledge of the rich plant and animal life that thrived here is based on fossils found by amateur palaeontologists like Red Deer's Betty Speirs. Through her work, and that of others from the University of Alberta, the Red Deer area has received international recognition for its variety of fossils and their excellent state of preservation. Fish, insects and other invertebrates, mammals, seeds, fruit, cones and leaves have all been found in exposures of the Paskapoo sandstone particularly at Burbank, near the bridge on Highway 11 east and along road cuts in the area.

WHERE ARE THE DINOSAUR FOSSILS?

ERA	PERIOD	EPOCH	AGE MILLION YEARS
CENOZOIC	Quaternary	Recent or Holocene	
		Pleistocene	2
	Tertiary	Pliocene	5
		Miocene	23
		Oligocene	37
		Eocene	55
		Paleocene	65
MESOZOIC	Cretaceous		140
	Jurassic		195
	Triassic		230
PALEOZOIC	Permian		280
	Carboniferous		345
	Devonian		400
	Silurian		435
	Ordovician		500
	Cambrian		600

Around Red Deer, bedrock of the Paskapoo Formation forms cliffs along the river or is thinly covered by glacial deposits of sand and gravel. Paskapoo sandstone is less than 65 million years old, placing it in the Tertiary Period of the geological time scale.

Below the Paskapoo, but not exposed, are older layers of rock. These older layers can be seen farther downstream near Trochu, in the Drumheller Valley and at Dinosaur Provincial Park. Dinosaurs died out near the end of the Cretaceous Period over 65 million years ago. To find their bones, you must travel to areas such as Drumheller and Dinosaur Provincial Park near Brooks where rocks from the Dinosaur Age are exposed.

Burbank, east of Blackfalds and downstream from Red Deer, was the site of the primeval backswamp. Aquatic insect fossils are common here but few fish fossils are found. A stagnating swamp, much like the sloughs of today, would not have had enough oxygen dissolved in the water to sustain fish. Along the edges of the swamp, horsetails, ferns and other water–loving plants grew, eventually leaving their imprints for us to find.

The sandstone layers near the Highway 11 bridge show small changes in the ancient landscape. Small lakes were common at some times, streams cut through the sand and silt in other seasons. The area was, however, generally wet. During years of high runoff, schools of smelt–like *Speirsaenigma lindoei* would swim into interconnected pools only to be stranded once the floodwaters receded. Large numbers of complete fish skeletons have been found, clues pointing to massive die–offs.

The shores of these lakes and rivers were lined by *Joffrea speirsii*, a broad–leaved tree that, like today's cottonwood, grew in the mud and probably required a large amount of moisture for sprouting and subsequent growth. Leaves, seeds and seedlings of this tree were also fossilized. Other trees common in this area included birches, Mexican elm, Chinese water pine, Joffre plane tree, willows and metasequoias (also known as dawn redwoods).

The sediments making up the Paskapoo sandstone were laid down during the Age of Mammals. The last of the dinosaurs had disappeared and this new group of creatures expanded rapidly into every ecological niche imaginable. Primates similar to modern lemurs, and small shrew–like insectivores were common. Usually, palaeontologists must try to reconstruct an entire animal from a few fossil jaw, tooth or bone fragments. Imagine their delight at finding an entire pantodont skeleton! The sandstone has given up fossils of a myriad of mammals, including ancestors of today's ungulates and carnivores. What is lacking are bird fossils, since delicate

bird bones were often destroyed long before they could be fossilized.

Hiking party on Hogsback in Red Deer River Canyon, c. 1920.
This cliff is an example of Paskapoo sandstone.

WHAT IS A FOSSIL?

On your next trip to a museum, take a close look at a fossil bone. If you are allowed to touch one, feel its smooth hardness. Does it feel like the bone from your Sunday roast? Is it heavier or lighter?

Such fossils are no longer bones. The original material was replaced by minerals. It might have happened like this: An animal died millions of years ago and collapsed in a swamp. The body did not decay as it was rapidly covered by layers of sediment: clay, silt and sand deposited by rivers or blown in by the wind. More and more sediment covered the body until the weight of layers created enough pressure for the lowest layers to turn to stone. At the same time, water may have seeped in and dissolved the bone, leaving only an imprint. Chemicals may have filled in the space occupied by the bone, producing an exact copy of the bone. Sometimes this chemical replacement is so slow, that minute details such as cell structures are preserved. In very fine sediments, the impressions of the soft parts—skin, feathers, entire bodies of invertebrates, leaves and flowers—can occasionally be found.

Fossil plants form in the same way. Fossils of animals and plants living near or in water are preserved more than any other. The chances of being covered quickly by sediment is far greater in a water environment where rivers are constantly depositing new sediments than on land where soil deposition is much slower.

Look for exposures of Paskapoo sandstone at the Maskepetoon cliffs across from Lower Heritage Ranch, below Cronquist Business Park opposite Bower Ponds, and by the River Bend Golf Course and Recreation Area. Canoeists and river rafters can also see a massive projection of sandstone at the Hogsback, downstream from the Canyon Ski Area in the Red Deer River Canyon.

Grasslands and Gravel

The Rockies, although over 200 kilometres away, continued to influence the landscapes of Central Alberta. They sent powerful, fast–flowing rivers onto the plains carrying huge quantities of cobbles, gravel, sand and silt. On the flatter plains, the rivers lost some of their energy and began dropping their load. Valleys and depressions were filled and obliterated. At other times, when more water rushed down the east slopes, old deposits were reworked and new valleys were carved.

These alternating periods of massive deposition and erosion went on for about 20 million years until about 45 million years ago when the major uplift of the mountains ended. The gravel beds deposited during this period, called the Saskatchewan or pre–glacial gravels, were left locally in beds up to four metres thick. These beds can be seen in the high cliffs below Maskepetoon Park, across the river from Bower Ponds and at River Bend. The gravel beds are made up almost exclusively of quartzite with some sandstone, limestone and local rock mixed in. Many of the huge sand and gravel deposits left behind are seeing the light of day once again in commercial sand and gravel mining operations throughout Central Alberta.

The ancestral Red Deer River carved its valley at this time. Difficult to see now around Red Deer, a drive to Blackfalds Lake places you right in the old river channel. The valley becomes even more evident near Ponoka where the river headed northeast and eventually joins with the ancestral North Saskatchewan River. The present Battle River follows much of the Red Deer's old, wide, deep valley.

During this time, the climate also changed. Temperatures slowly dropped and the sub–tropical climate became more like the continental climate of today. Ferns died out and were replaced by deciduous and coniferous trees. The land became drier and grasslands dominated.

Mammals adjusted quickly to their changing world. Ungulates (hoofed animals) grazed the plains in large numbers. Huge rhinoceroses of the genus *Dicatherium* roamed in herds. The first horses and camels, then about the size of foxes, left a rich evolutionary record tracing their development to the forms we know today. The lush plant life supported an explosion of new life forms with many 'gigantics'—huge bison, mammoths, woolly rhinoceroses, sabre–toothed cats, beavers, bears and sloths—appearing and thriving before the arrival of the Ice Age. Their bones are buried in the pre–glacial gravels.

The ancestral Red Deer River carved a narrow, steep-walled valley in some places, a wide, gentle-sloping valley in others. Here the Chain Lakes occupy the former riverbed.

The hills and hollows of this glacially-landscaped terrain provide excellent habitat for wildlife.

The Big Chill

Ice—kilometres thick. Huge sheets of ice slowly creeping southwestward from the Canadian Shield and eastward from the mountains. At Red Deer, they met. Together, they headed south.

Glaciers and ice sheets, by their very nature, erase much of their own history. Ice plucks and scours rock, then drags the rock to its journey's end. As one ice sheet advances over the route of its ancestor, it obliterates virtually all evidence of the first glacier's passage.

Central Alberta has been glaciated may times in the last two million years. The last of the ice sheets, the Wisconsin, so named because it reached as far as today's State of Wisconsin, arrived about 30,000 years ago and disappeared about 12,000 years ago. The ice reached thicknesses of up to 1600 metres. It brought granite and gneiss from the north, limestone from the west and mixed these rocks with local sandstone, coal, petrified wood, shale and pre–glacial gravels. As had its predecessors, it scraped the land flat then dropped a seven to 30 metre-thick carpet of rock, called *till*, as it melted.

When large chunks of ice break from a glacier, they slowly melt in place, often insulated by a mantle of the rock they have carried. Debris is left all around them, and when the chunks of ice finally melt, rolling hills pocked with water–filled depressions result. This type of kame and kettle topography is easy to see between Delburne and Elnora from Highway 21, between Joffre and Stettler along Highway 911, and south of Stettler to Rowley on Highway 56.

15

Melting glacial waters pooled in low–lying areas. A huge lake formed around Red Deer stretching at times from Innisfail to Ponoka. The lake slowly crept northward, following the retreating ice sheet. The swollen river built huge deltas into the lake, dropping its load of rock, gravel and sand. One such delta underlies the Red Deer College grounds and the surrounding area. These sand hills are especially visible where sand and gravel mining have taken place next to Highway 2, and where Highway 2A cuts through the hills.

The biggest change to the landscape wrought by ice was the diversion of the Red Deer River. During pre–glacial times, the Red Deer flowed into the North Saskatchewan River. At some time during the Ice Age, the river's course was blocked by ice. The river turned 90 degrees to the east and flowed along the glacier's edge. It hesitated when it reached Divide Hill, then carved a new valley 140 metres deep in places. The western slope of this valley is now home to the Canyon Ski Hill. The Red Deer River today follows this channel southeast until it empties into the South Saskatchewan River near Empress close to the Alberta–Saskatchewan border.

Life flourished between the glacial advances. Grasslands and wetlands supported the giants of pre–glacial times. However, no bones have been found since they would have been broken and crushed by later advances of the ice.

The Red Deer River Canyon. This area was once proposed as the site of a national park.

Opposite: Point bar at Heritage Ranch taken from Maskepetoon cliffs.

Water, the Master Sculptor

The last glacial advance sculpted the land into the basic form we see today. Rolling hills, water–filled depressions such as Buffalo and Sylvan lakes, flat glacial lakebeds near Ponoka and Penhold, and the western foothills provide a diverse backdrop for the evolution of a variety of ecosystems. The land is not static, however. In the last 10,000 years or so, water, and to a lesser degree, wind, have modified the landscape, smoothing sharp edges, filling in hollows and softening the irregularities of the earth's skin.

Water is the major agent of erosion and deposition in Central Alberta. Rivers and streams, when running full and fast, have the power to carve deep into their banks and beds, exposing new layers of rock in their valley walls and changing their course. Banks are undercut, weakening the rock layers and causing slumps and slides. The sediments released in these events are transported by the speeding waters to curves of the river or widenings of the river channel where they are deposited when the water's headlong rush is checked.

Sediments, dropped when the water turns a corner and slows, eventually form a point bar. This tongue of sand, silt and gravel gradually grows larger and pushes farther into the river. The bar is slowly colonized by willows and sedges, plants that thrive in wet areas.

Once a watercourse reaches flatter ground, it loses its ability to cut deeper, and instead begins to loop back and forth across the valley floor. It continues to cut into one bank and deposit sediments by the other, forming ever–larger meander loops. Meander loops can be readily seen along Piper and Waskasoo creeks at the south end of Red Deer. In times of high water, the water may breach the neck of the loop. Once floodwaters subside, the river may change its course by abandoning the old loop and using the new, shorter channel.

The old river channel, now replenished only during periods of high water, is called an oxbow lake. The Gaetz Lakes are an example of an oxbow lake, cut in two by a landslide. As the river has continued to cut down into its bed, it has left the Gaetz Lakes perched three or more metres above the river level. Most oxbow lakes slowly dry up and fill with plant remains. During their lifetime, they are prime wildlife areas. Cattails and bulrushes, as well as other water plants, grow in their still, shallow waters. These plants, in turn, provide nesting and hiding sites for ducks and shorebirds and food for beaver, muskrat and moose. As

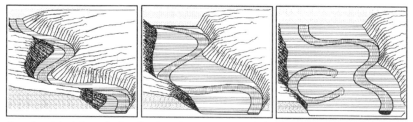

An oxbow lake is formed when the river changes course and abandons a meander loop.

open water is gradually choked by sedges, grasses and willows, deer, snowshoe hare and numerous rodents take advantage of the growing feast. Eventually a wet meadow results with a ring of encroaching poplars. The Gaetz Lakes are fed by both springs and Gaetz Creek, and so haven't met their ultimate fate as quickly as they might have if they depended only on floods to refill them.

Life of a River

The power of a river is determined by the amount of water that flows into it and the gradient of the land over which it travels. The Red Deer River rises in the Rocky Mountains in the wilderness of Banff National Park, west of Lake Louise. Its upper reaches, some of which can be accessed from the Forestry Trunk Road, are characterized by rapids loved by whitewater canoeists and rafters. It pitches and rolls over bedrock shelves and huge boulders, scouring deep overhung pockets into limestone cliffs. Its ferocity lessens as it leaves the foothills and spills onto the plains. Before long, however, it is throttled by the Dickson Dam, and now tamed, flows meekly toward Red Deer and the plains.

Before the dam was built, the Red Deer was a much different river than the one we know today. In spring its waters rose, pushing ice up the banks and scraping and scouring the trees. Ice pans jammed against the bridge supports. Residents would watch the groaning ice and hold their breath, wondering which would go first, the ice or the bridge. Usually the ice jam broke before any bridge supports were knocked out. But not always. The original Gaetz Avenue traffic bridges were swept away by ice and the Canadian National Railway abandoned its bridge at the mouth of Waskasoo Creek because of repeated ice damage.

Rain also swelled the river, causing it to surge over the banks and flood lower-lying areas, both in the city and in the country. It cleaned the riverbanks of logs and debris, carrying them to the next point bar or even farther downstream. As the river reached the badlands, it uncovered ancient animals encased in the rock and washed away the grey bentonite clay.

Flood on the Red Deer River just east from Gaetz Avenue. April 4, 1943.

As spring turned into summer, the waters subsided, leaving only ice–scoured trees, sediment-covered river flats and flotsam suspended in willow branches as evidence of its earlier fury. The waters continued to drop through the warmth of the summer and by fall, islands and gravel bars would begin to appear.

Today the river is domesticated. The dam was built to maintain a constant flow of water through Red Deer year–round, to meet the water needs of a growing city and to ensure a sufficient quantity of water in the winter to absorb the treated sewage pumped into the river. The dam prevents some spring floods, holding back snowmelt and rain water that once swelled the Red Deer. The dam has no influence, however, on rain and snowmelt that enter the river downstream. The river still rises and pans of ice are jammed into the river's curves, but bridges, homes and farmers' fields are safe most years. Water levels are lower than before through the summer, and higher in fall and winter as the water is released slowly from the reservoir. There are still fluctuations in the water level, but some of the peaks and lows in the flow are gone.

While the dam may be a boon to humanity, it has contributed little to the river environment. Cottonwoods that once shaded the riverbanks are dying and this magnificent tree is gradually disappearing along the Red Deer River. Cottonwood seeds need damp, fresh soil in which to germinate. Young seedlings depend on spring floods for nutrients from silt and water during their first few years of growth, until their root systems become well established. With the high water peaks virtually eliminated, the old cottonwoods are succumbing to old age and few young trees are there to replace them.

The ice breakups in the past scoured the banks and river bottom. Now the ice melts in place, dropping its silt load onto the bottom where it accumulates year after year. The silt and the clearer water encourage the growth of thick mats of algae and plankton, which cover the spawning grounds of fish like sculpin. Many of these fish species have vanished from the river below the dam.

Floods carried nutrients from the fields and forests that they invaded, back into the river. The lack of this food for fish and aquatic insects has impoverished the river.

The change in the water flow has changed the water temperature as well. Water caught in the reservoir reaches a uniform temperature: in summer, the water is colder than shallower, sun–warmed flowing waters. In winter, reservoir waters released into the river are several degrees warmer than the ice–cold natural flow. This greatly affects the fish populations. Mountain whitefish, for instance, spawn earlier in the year now in the warmer water of winter's end, but once the young emerge, the summer waters stay cooler than normal. The cooler water decreases their growth rate and ability to feed. Very few survive.

The dam itself prevents trout from moving upstream to spawn. Bull trout have disappeared and most trout caught in the lower Red Deer River were placed there by government fish stocking programs.

The scars on huge poplar trees, once made by ice scraping against the trunks, are never reopened these days. The sediment swept from the mountains is dropped behind the wall of the dam. Erosion continues, but at a lesser rate with fewer surges of water to carry the sediments and to build new point bars. Like most of Alberta's rivers, the Red Deer is no longer wild.

Bower Ponds.

The Parkland Mosaic

Red Deer lies in the heart of a parkland battleground, a witness to a struggle eons old—a war sometimes won by the aspen groves, sometimes by the grasslands. Today, the aspens are winning, but it was not always like that.

The aspen parkland is a natural region that girds Alberta like a belt. An area of about 60,000 square kilometres, it sweeps across the middle 10% to 15% of the province. To the north lies the boreal forest region, to the south and east, the grasslands and, to the west, the foothills. A distinctive assemblage of plant and animal species thrives in each region.

The aspen parkland is unique because it shares animals and plants from all three neighbouring regions. It is a transition zone, what a biologist calls an ecotone, between grassland and forest. From the air it looks like a patchwork quilt with interlocking pieces coloured different shades of blue and green by rivers, lakes, sloughs, aspen groves, spruce forests, grassy meadows, and crop– and range lands.

This living patchwork changes from year to year. Before European settlement, the battles between aspen groves and grasslands were both fierce and subtle. Prairie fires from lightning strikes or deliberately set by native people periodically darkened the skies with smoke and killed invading aspens. Herds of bison trampled young trees and brush, making room for the advance of the grasslands. After each setback, the aspens resumed their trek southward, sending long roots into the grasslands from which sprouted young saplings. Birds and small mammals were unwitting soldiers eating the seeds of aspen and shrubs then scattering them, wrapped in rich fertilizer, on the freshly dug soil near ground squirrel holes.

The settlers arrived. They plowed the grasslands, but in the days of horse power, large stands of trees were left untouched. Fires were the settler's greatest enemy, threatening lives, livestock and homes; anyone caught setting fires and leaving them unattended was hauled off by the North West Mounted Police to be tried and punished. Farmers plowed and maintained fire guards, a wide swath of soil that they left unseeded, around their fields. A wild fire could not leap over this bare ground. Grass fires were quickly put out. Where untouched parkland remained, the aspen slowly engulfed the grasslands.

> **CONTROLLED BURNS**
>
> In many protected areas—Alberta's national parks, for example—fires are deliberately set to reduce the fire hazard from dead wood and to improve the habitat for wildlife. This is not a new concept: the native peoples of the prairies regularly set fires to ensure grazing for their number one resource, the bison. Spring fires promoted grass growth while beating back the encroaching aspens.

The use of the tractor in farming rapidly destroyed the aspen parkland.

Subduing the forest was difficult work and most farm fields ended where the trees began. This changed after the Second World War. Tractors, once the workhorses of the rich, were now mass produced and could be afforded by everyone. The machines could do in minutes what once took days of backbreaking labour. Pitted against bulldozers and tractors, the trees lost. The destruction of the aspen parkland had begun.

A few large tracts of aspen parkland are still found in Central Alberta. Most are within parks and designated natural areas or where glaciers left rolling hills difficult to plow. Smaller expanses are found on farms and along rivers where long fingers of parkland continue to invade the surrounding boreal forest, foothills and grasslands.

A rich variety of plants and animals call the aspen parkland home. To the beaver, the aspen parkland is a marsh, slough, lake or river fringed by willows, water birch, aspen poplar and balsam poplar. This large rodent thrives throughout the region, finding food in the bark, leaves and young branches of these trees, and building materials in their thicker branches and trunks.

Hunted to the point of extinction for its fur, the beaver has made a solid comeback. Today, most bodies of water host at least one pair. Even a small stream is a potential home, once this master engineer sets to work. A dam of sticks and mud, well anchored in the streambed and stretching from bank to bank, captures water and creates a deep pool.

THE ASPEN WOODS

Is it one tree or a hundred? Aspen poplars reproduce through seeds and by sending up suckers from their roots. City dwellers curse the little trees that pop up through their lawn and foresters treat them like weeds, but for the aspen, this type of growth ensures its survival. An aspen grove spreads rapidly from a central parent tree, taking advantage of good growing conditions. Take a look in the fall: since all the clones are genetically identical, they all change colour at the same time. Thus a forest will have patches of aspens with yellow leaves, while others are still green. In the spring, all the interconnected trees leaf out at the same time.

ASPEN OR BALSAM?

These two poplars are common deciduous trees in the aspen parkland. Of the two poplars, the aspen is the most prevalent, growing in dry areas, in large pure stands or mixed with balsam or spruce. The aspen is often called the trembling aspen. Take a close look at the leaf: the stalk is flattened and thin. The leaf flutters in the slightest breeze.

Balsam poplar grow best in damper areas, often lining riverbanks or lakes and sloughs. The balsam poplar leaf is larger and heart–shaped with a substantial stalk. In winter, warm the leaf bud in your hand to smell the heady fragrance of the balsam's resin.

Balsam poplar on the left, aspen poplar on the right.

Once the water is deep enough not to freeze to the bottom, the beaver directs its energy to the building of a dome–shaped lodge with an underwater entrance. Where banks are not too hard, beavers will dig burrows extending up to 10 metres under the surrounding forest. As fall approaches, the beaver anchors a cache of twigs and branches underwater near the lodge entrance to ensure a food supply for the winter when it is imprisoned under the ice.

The beaver shares its pond with many neighbours. Muskrat, smaller and with a long, thin tail, scour the bottom in search of cattail roots. They bulldoze cattails and bulrushes into conical heaps near the edges of the water, excavate a chamber in each, and prepare for the winter. A summer den is built in the same way. Unlike the beaver's lodge, the muskrat's huts last only one season.

Neither muskrat nor beaver are completely safe in their watery world. Mink often scout the edges of water bodies for these animals as well as for young birds and frogs. Coyote, lynx and fox will attempt to surprise a beaver intent on felling a tree; muskrat fall prey to owls, hawks and even pike.

The beaver's endeavours often flood low–lying areas and produce expansive wetlands where cattails, sedges, bulrushes and water

DEER

Both mule (left) and white–tailed (right) deer are common in the aspen parkland. The mule deer sports huge ears and a white rump with a short, black–tipped tail. The white–tailed deer covers its white rump with a longer, broad tail. When alarmed, this deer raises and waves its tail like a flag to signal danger. The antlers of the mule deer fork; the points on a white–tail's antlers all grow from a main beam.

plants quickly take root. These areas, in turn, attract moose and waterfowl. Flotillas of coots, grebes, mallards and other ducks loaf in the open waters, kept open by muskrat feeding on plant roots. Food—aquatic plants and insects—is plentiful. Plant stems swaying above the water provide shelter from storms and anchoring places for nests. Red–winged and yellow–headed blackbirds bind their nests part way up the taller stems.

Beaver canals and trails push into the tangle of willow, red osier dogwood, river alder and water birch perched at the edge of marshes and wet meadows. Favourite browse for moose and deer as well as beaver, these shrubs rapidly give way to saskatoon, chokecherry and silverberry on drier ground.

This belt of marsh vegetation and shrubs is rich habitat for birds and a frustration to bird watchers. Startlingly bright goldfinch and yellow warbler disappear into the shrubs in the blink of an eye. Alder flycatcher dart out to grab a passing insect, then they too vanish. A trained ear soon picks out the trill of the song sparrow, the *bzzzzz* of the clay–coloured sparrow and the bubbling musical song of the marsh wren. Look overhead for the springtime dives of long–beaked snipes and, along muddy shores, for skittering sandpipers, avocet and yellowlegs probing for buried insects.

Beyond the margins of the wetland is the aspen forest. Here deer blend into the underbrush made up of saskatoon, red osier dogwood, beaked hazelnut, buffaloberry, snowberry, willow and wild rose. As well as acting as cover, such bushes provide food for both mule and white–tailed deer. These browsers nip off the buds and young branches of the shrubs. Grasses, wildflowers, mushrooms and even lichens round out their diet.

Deer give birth to one or two fawns in late May or early June. The young are hidden in bush or deep grass where they lie still and quiet to prevent detection by predatory coyotes or bears. The doe returns to nurse the fawns periodically. Only after about three weeks do the fawns join their mother on feeding forays.

Deer have many neighbours in the aspen woodlands. Snowshoe hare beat down extensive trail systems through the underbrush to make travel, and escape from enemies, fast and easy. In summer, bushes grow in bowers over these trails; in winter, hard–packed snow and distinctive hare tracks make these runways very visible. The trails connect feeding areas where the hares gnaw the bark off shrubs or nibble their tips.

A hare's speed, coat colour and alertness saves it from its enemies. Should a coyote or a lynx approach, the hare may crouch and freeze. It depends on the colour of its coat—brown in summer and white in winter—for concealment. If spied, the hare launches from its hiding place and with great erratic leaps, tries to outdistance and outmanoeuvre its hunter. If a coyote, fox, lynx or owl still manages to close in, the hare increases its speed to up to 50 kilometres per hour. Chased by a single animal the hare usually wins, but when faced by a coyote and its concealed mate, the hare may not be so lucky.

The hare has some respite in the spring when many predators turn their attention to other prey: the young of almost every animal and adult male grouse. The ruffed grouse, found in aspen and spruce forests, stays close to a favourite log during the spring. From its perch on this drumming log, the male grouse displays for

A hare disappears into the woods.

passing females. It fluffs out its neck ruff, spreads its tail feathers, then beats its wings rapidly to make a booming sound. This sound carries through the forest and attracts females for mating, and alerts predators. Should danger approach, the grouse stays perfectly still, then suddenly, explodes into flight. It may alight in the safety of a tree nearby or continue its low flight for a short distance before landing and running through the underbrush.

Such dramas rarely go un–noticed. The black–billed magpie is the town crier of the aspen parkland. Once a constant companion of the bison herds, the magpie, too, nearly disappeared. Its ability to adapt to settlement has allowed it to increase its numbers and spread from grassland to parkland. The magpie is a scavenger ever alert to predators entering the forest, warning all with its raucous squawks. Its sharp eyes spot carrion, insects, eggs and other delicacies to fill its gizzard or to take back to its young. Perched high in an aspen or a spruce, the magpie's nest resembles a scraggly bundle of sticks haphazardly arranged into a ball. Inside this hollow structure lies the magpie's feather–lined mud nest. The nest is used primarily during the summer but may shelter its builder on very cold days in winter. Once abandoned, the nest is eagerly adopted by red squirrels or may form the base for a hawk's nest.

The magpie is equally at home in the spruce forest. Aspen woods give way to white spruce on shady riverbanks, north–facing slopes, and cool damp hollows and river flats, mixing briefly to produce a rich forest with a variety of plant and animal species. As aspens grow, they provide shade needed for spruce seedlings to develop. As the poplars reach old age, at about 75 to 100 years and 23 to 30 metres in height, they begin to succumb to fungus and disease. The spruce then become the dominant trees in the forest. Young spruce find the cool, shady and slightly acidic soil below these evergreens a perfect place to grow. Unless a fire sweeps through the forest and kills the spruce, these trees will continue to spread by seed.

The red squirrel is an unknowing spruce gardener. When looking for food to store for the winter, the squirrel makes the spruce its

TAMARACK SWAMP

Sandwiched between the Red Deer River and Highway 2 is a pocket of forest deserving special protection. This stand of tamaracks is separated from its kin by roads, fields, towns and climate. Tamaracks generally grow farther north and west where the climate is cooler and wetter. Tucked against a north slope, these tamaracks have found a small piece of paradise with just the right conditions. But for how long?

The tamarack is a deciduous conifer, that is, a cone–bearing tree like a spruce or a pine, that also loses its leaves every fall like an aspen or other leafy tree. The needles grow in tufts, giving the tree a soft look. In September, the needles turn gold and by October the trees are usually bare. Tamaracks grow in wet places where there is a constant, if almost imperceptible, flow of water past their roots. How long Red Deer's tamarack swamp, and the unusual orchids and other rare plants it shelters, will survive no one knows; the effect of the highway and railway construction on the groundwater flow so important to the tamarack's survival is not yet clear.

Tamarack grow in the muskegs west of Rocky Mountain House on land they share with black spruce. Walking through these areas is an adventure; the ground feels like thick, waterlogged foam and hungry mosquitos abound. These, and the tamarack swamps near Morningside, are wonderful to look at in the fall.

Red Deer's tamarack swamp has long been a favourite haunt for naturalists. Forays into its heart yielded new and rare species of plants, animals and insects. These observations were published nationally in both popular and scientific magazines in the early 1900s.

supermarket. As the cones ripen, squirrels gnaw their stems, sending the cones plummeting to the forest floor. One squirrel may harvest 14,000 cones in a single season! Most will be gathered and hidden while others will be forgotten and may sprout in place.

A squirrel has a few favourite eating places within its territories. These are easy to find—just look for a heap of cone scales and stems on the ground, then look up. Chances are that the squirrel will be perched on a branch, already scolding you for your intrusion. The garbage heap, or midden, grows from year to year, and may be used by several generations. It is riddled with tunnels and chambers and when the temperature drops below –25° C, the current owner retreats into this maze to nibble away its food stocks in warmth and quiet.

A mature spruce forest is a cathedral–like place. Very little light filters through the heavy boughs. The air is still; any wind is caught by the tree tops. Snow, too, is caught in the uppermost branches, and little reaches the ground. Few plants grow in this dark, cool environment. Those that do, such as the twin–flower, bunchberry, one–sided wintergreen and various feather mosses and lichens, hug the forest floor. By no means barren, the spruce forest nevertheless offers little that is attractive to mammals. Flying squirrels glide from branch to branch on sail–like flaps of skin extending from their front to their back legs. Snowshoe hare visit on occasion to nibble the buds and bark of seedlings while deer use the woods as a winter highway, unimpeded by the light snow cover.

A walk through the spruce woods engages all the senses. In summer, the resin or sap oozing through a cut in the bark scents the woods. Cool air contrasts with the heat of the grasslands and open aspen forest. Golden–crowned and ruby–crowned kinglets scoot from tree to tree, while red–breasted nuthatches stride, headfirst, down the tree trunks, probing under the bark for insects.

In winter, the spruce forest is hushed, with only the crackle of the snow underfoot. At least until you are noticed by a magpie or a blue jay! Both are common residents of the spruce forest. The blue jay, loud and aggressive during the winter months, disappears from sight in the summer. Although these jays nest in conifers, they are quiet and secretive until the young can forage on their own.

The spruce forest is an important wintering ground for birds such as blue jay, nuthatches, brown creeper, crossbills and woodpeckers. Curious black–capped and boreal chickadees converge to inspect any

intruder. Except for the blue jay, which often scavenges, most birds wintering among the spruce are insect eaters. The nuthatches, creepers and chickadees investigate every cranny and crack for dormant insects. Crossbills, with their misaligned bill, are superbly adapted to plucking seeds out of cones. Woodpeckers drill holes into old standing trees in search of boring insects under the bark or carpenter ants within the trunk. Their long, bristled, sticky tongues snatch fleeing bugs from their tunnels.

Blue jays leave the spruce woods to fill their crops with sunflower seeds from backyard bird feeders.

In contrast to the spruce woods are

31

the grassland areas of the parkland. The grasslands are the domain of the Richardson's ground squirrel—commonly called a gopher. This small rodent thrives in open areas among native grasses such as rough fescue, June grass, wheat grass and spear grass, and adapts readily to pastures and formal lawns. Where grasses grow tall, ground squirrels clip trails from their den mouth to favourite feeding spots. These groomed trails are vital for quick escapes from the ground squirrel's numerous enemies: coyote, red fox, weasel, badger, hawks, and even domestic dogs and cats.

Ground squirrels live in colonies. Safety in numbers is an excellent practice for ground squirrels: the more members there are to a colony, the more eyes there are to spot predators. Although they live in groups, ground squirrels are not social animals. Each defends its territory against trespassers. The exception is family members. A mother, while maintaining her own territory, will live near her daughters and sisters. The males, however, move out at maturity to join a colony of non–relatives. In this way, in–breeding is reduced.

Male ground squirrels are the first to enter hibernation, usually by the end of June. They are also the first to wake and may be active as early as February in southern Alberta. The males establish their territories long before the females come out of hibernation in April or early May, and defend them fiercely. The females bear their young only 24 days after mating. The young first leave the burrow at five weeks to find grass, insects and carrion on their own. They continue to share the burrow with their mother until they reach adult size in late summer. Once the breeding season is over, the males are less aggressive and spend most of their time eating to prepare for their eight month hibernation. Adult females are usually underground by late July and only the young of the year who haven't yet put on enough fat reserves are still above ground.

An Altered Landscape

The aspen parkland is now the exception rather than the rule in Central Alberta. The fertile soils and favourable climate were not lost on farmers coming to settle in Western Canada at the turn of the century. Since then, the treed plains have succumbed to the bulldozer and the plow, leaving a much different landscape.

Farms in the parkland average about 200 hectares in size, smaller than the Alberta average but far more productive. Some farmers only grow grain, others raise cattle. Mixed farms, where both grain and cattle are produced, are quite common.

Fields of Grain

A leisurely drive in the country in July and August will take you past fields of barley, wheat, oats, canola, fava beans, alfalfa and speciality crops. Barley is the number one grain, accounting for almost half of the crops grown here. Look for wind–rippled fields with a slight purplish tinge. The tightly clustered seedheads are bewhiskered with long bristles. The best of the barley is used for malting while the rest goes for livestock feed. Wheat, grown for flour to make bread, cereal, pasta and related products, has a large seedhead but without the bristles.

Canola, sometimes known as rapeseed, carpets the fields with sunshine in July. This bright yellow flower produces tiny black seeds that are crushed for their rich, low cholesterol oil. Check your cupboard—your cooking oil may be canola oil! The crushed seeds are fed to cattle while some birders buy the whole seeds to feed goldfinches, redpolls and other small wild birds.

Most other fields, about 22% of surrounding lands, are either pasture or growing hay. Hay can be just alfalfa, but more commonly includes a mixture of different grasses with the alfalfa. Depending on the mixture, the hay will be fed to cattle or horses. The hay is harvested twice; once in the middle of the summer and once in early fall. The second cut is considered the better of the two with a higher protein content.

Some grain crops are harvested specifically for silage. The plants are chopped up, then piled in huge heaps or in pits and covered with plastic. The silage is like a big compost heap with the plant materials heating up in the damp environment of the pit. In poor years when crops have been damaged by hail, have not matured properly or when fields are weed infested, the year's production can be salvaged by turning it into silage to feed to cattle.

Speciality crops are also grown to diversify farms from one crop to several. Fava beans, mustards, strawberries, saskatoons, vegetables, honey, flowers for drying and herbs can all be found. Numerous farms now offer u–pick opportunities, a chance to choose your own produce while enjoying the fresh country air and fighting off a mosquito or two.

Beast and Bird Down on the Farm

Beef cattle are the other main 'crop' in the area, about 100,000 of them. The main ones are Herefords (white face with a red body), Black or Red Angus (slightly smaller in size than other cattle and all one colour), Charolais (white), Simmental (red and white), Limousin (red), Gelbveigh (light red), Salers (dark red) and Maine Anjou (deep red with a white belly). Driving by the farm gate and checking for a sign advertising the farm's speciality is often the easiest way to find out the type of beast that is grazing in the field!

Dairy farms can be picked out by looking for black and white Holsteins. Other milk cows such as Jerseys and Guernseys are few in number and usually serve as the milk and butter providers for a family, rather than in a commercial operation.

Large and small hog farms are scattered throughout Central Alberta. Some hogs may be seen wandering in corrals but most are kept indoors in long, low metal buildings. Chickens and turkeys are often raised in similar buildings. Heavily fenced fields keep sheep and goats in and coyotes and stray dogs out.

Horses are a common sight in the area as well. Most are used for farm work or pleasure riding, but breeds like Arabians, Quarter Horses and Morgans are not uncommon. Large draught horses, Standardbreds, Tennessee Walkers, Paso Finos and other breeds can also be seen.

More and more farmers, in an attempt to diversify their farms, are looking at different types of livestock. Speciality farms raise llamas, alpacas, ostriches, rheas, emus, angora goats, donkeys, and a variety of small exotic fowl and rabbits.

To Market, To Market...

Grain leaves the parkland in special rounded boxcars for markets across Canada, the United States, Europe and Asia. In the fall, farm grain bins are filled to bursting with the golden seeds. After bumper crops, heaps of grain are stockpiled in fields until they can be transported to the nearest grain elevator for grading and shipping.

Cattle are either bought straight off the farm, or in most cases, at auctions. Auction marts are located in any town of any size and usually hold a weekly livestock auction. These auctions are both entertaining and educational; if you can follow the auctioneer's patter and eavesdrop on neighbours discussing the current livestock prices, you can gain a new perspective on farming in the 1990s.

Exotic animals are bought off the farm or featured in special events presented specifically to showcase the breed. Odd and Unusual Sales are often held to sell some of the smaller animals.

Farmer's markets, country fairs, homecomings and rodeos are colourful and entertaining showcases for vegetables, fruit, baked goods and crafts produced down on the farm. Information centres maintain a list of events and when they are held.

The Faces of Central Alberta

For over 10,000 years, people have left clues to their journeys across Central Alberta. These clues—stone tools, fragments of butchered bone, charcoal from ancient fires, heat–shattered rock—are pieced together to tell the story of nomadic peoples. Mammoths, giant camels and huge bison were killed by small groups of hunters using spears. For centuries after the retreat of the great ice sheets, these animals grazed on the lush grasslands growing in their wake, then, for reasons not yet fully understood, these gigantics disappeared. The hunters turned their attention to the smaller animals that had evolved—bison, elk and deer—animals more familiar to us today.

The transition from hunting with spears to bows and arrows is marked by changes in the size and shape of the stone points. As the hunting technology changed, so did living patterns. The small family groups of 10,000 years ago slowly evolved into extended family groups, then small bands that would hunt co–operatively and share their kills. By approximately 1,800 years ago, native people had developed new strategies for hunting bison by driving them over cliffs or into pounds (corrals). Large quantities of meat could be procured this way, so larger gatherings of people were possible.

Bison jumps and their associated meat processing and campsites are usually rich in artifacts. These jumps were used repeatedly over many centuries or millennia, but were relatively few in number. What are more

---

DRY ISLAND BUFFALO JUMP

The cliffs of Dry Island Buffalo Jump Provincial Park tower serenely over the Red Deer River. Many times over the last two thousand years, these cliffs have provided native people with vast amounts of bison meat, hides, horns and other important bison parts.

A scout located a nearby bison herd, and then brave young hunters, disguised in bison hides and coyote skins, lured the herd toward the cliff. Swift runners or mounted hunters stampeded the animals. Camp members hidden behind lines of piled stones rose as the herd thundered by, frightening them further, encouraging their blind rush toward the valley edge. By the time the animals saw the 50 metre drop it was too late; with the panicked herd pressing from behind, the animals had no choice but to plunge over the lip and fall to their deaths.

As the last animal landed at the base, more hunters rushed in to dispatch those animals that had only been crippled in the fall. The women, assisted by children and the old folks, butchered the animals. Tongues and the fat–rich humps were delicacies to be eaten that night. Other meat was roasted or sliced into thin strips and dried. All that could be used before it spoiled was removed from the kill site and moved to the campsite near the river. The rest provided a feast for wolves, prairie grizzly bears, coyotes, turkey vultures and numerous other scavengers attracted by the noise and the smell of blood.

numerous are campsites. Campsites were used only for a period of one night or a few days. The remains found at these sites are often sparse, so campsites are much more difficult to find. Many have been lost to the plow or urban development. The first Europeans to arrive in Central Alberta recorded their observations of the native peoples they found. After about 1720, the Blackfoot lived south of the Red Deer River, wresting the territory from the Shoshone (Snake). And before them? No one really knows: the stories passed down through the generations by native peoples refer to these ancient people as the Old Ones, or not at all. Archaeological evidence paints a picture of a way of life but only hints at the origin of the campers.

In Search of Fur
The fur traders were the first Europeans to venture into this area. Anthony Henday in 1754, followed by Peter Fidler in 1792 and David Thompson in 1799, were searching for furs and people to supply them to the fur trade companies. Unlike the Cree living north of the Red Deer River, the traders found the Blackfoot not terribly interested in trapping beaver and other mammals to supply Europeans hungry for felt hats and fur coats. After their initial disappointment, the traders found another use for the people of the parkland and the prairie: as suppliers of bison meat, pemmican and hides.

The traders moved farther west, finally settling on a site near the North Saskatchewan River now known as Rocky Mountain House. There, in 1799, the Hudson Bay Company (HBC) and the North West Company founded rival forts. They hoped to capture the trade of the Kootenay from across the Rocky Mountains, but the Kootenays, sworn enemies of the Blackfoot, never ventured into their enemy's territory. Instead, the forts catered to the Blackfoot and the Stoneys.

The fierce fighting between the rival companies resulted in bloodshed and low profits. Finally, in 1821, the two companies merged under the Hudson Bay Company name. The North West Company post was abandoned and Acton House, the HBC post, remained active until 1835. Never very profitable, the post closed, only to be opened again years later before being permanently abandoned in 1875.

While the post did not bring in a fortune of furs as had been hoped, it did serve as a base for explorations to the west. From Rocky Mountain House, David Thompson set off in 1807 to find a trade route across the mountains. Howse Pass seemed an ideal route for reaching the Kootenay. The Peigan, a member of the Blackfoot Confederacy, blockaded the route to prevent the Kootenay from obtaining rifles. In 1810, Thompson turned northward and blazed a new trade route from Fort Edmonton to the Athabasca River and through Athabasca Pass. This discovery further reduced the need for a post at Rocky Mountain House.

Koo Koo Sint—He Who Looks at Stars

David Thompson—fur trader, explorer, mapmaker. The man who drew the first detailed map of Western Canada, a map that was to be used for over 100 years, arrived in Canada to apprentice for the Hudson Bay Company as a clerk. His duties took him from Churchill, Manitoba to Cumberland House in Saskatchewan. There he met Phillip Turnor, the HBC's chief surveyor. Turnor taught Thompson to read the stars and showed him how to survey the land. He sparked in the 17 year–old Thompson a desire to map the wilderness of Western Canada.

After a three–year stint as a HBC surveyor, Thompson joined the rival North West Company. The energetic young explorer was assigned tasks that appealed to his sense of adventure and made better use of his skills. During his long association with the North West Company, Thompson explored and mapped the major western waterways, established new trading areas and blazed a new route through the Rocky Mountains.

You can retrace his steps by following Highway 11, the David Thompson Highway, to Rocky Mountain House National Historic Park and onwards to the mountains. Backpackers may want to follow Thompson's routes to British Columbia over the Howse Pass in Banff National Park or to Athabasca Pass in Jasper National Park.

Mount Conway at Howse Pass.

THE MISSIONARIES

The fur traders had a profound impact on the native people's way of life. So did the missionaries. The Reverend Robert Rundle, Father Albert Lacombe, Father Constantine Scollen and the Reverends George and John McDougall travelled among the native camps and villages to convert native people to Christianity. These men were well respected by the people they came to teach and were often consulted in matters that dealt with the white outsiders. In the late 1800s, clergymen like Fathers Lacombe and Scollen were instrumental in maintaining order among natives during the Northwest Rebellion and, later, easing the transition from total freedom to reservation life.

The McDougalls were active in the Red Deer area. They ministered to native peoples from Fort Edmonton to their mission at Morley (between today's Calgary and Banff), travelling between the two settlements on the Wolf Track, a trail that crossed the Red Deer River at the ford (Fort Normandeau) west of the present city.

Two of Alberta's most important missionaries: the Reverend George McDougall on the left and the Reverend John McDougall on the right.

Thumbs Up for Agriculture

While the fur traders and the native peoples were dickering over furs and bison meat in the west, the British Government was setting new directions in the east. Threatened by encroachment by Americans from the south, the government wished to know the state, and worth, of its possessions beyond the Red River Settlement in Manitoba. In 1857, Captain John Palliser mounted an expedition to assess the prairies for their agricultural potential. He reported that while the southern prairies were far too arid for agriculture, the lands near the Red Deer River were fertile and rich in wildlife. This favourable report was expected to attract farmers to the area in droves by the 1870s. The expected flood was just a trickle, but it set the course for the years to come.

The End of the Bison Herds

Already the native peoples were searching longer and travelling farther to find bison to hunt. Métis people who had established winter villages in the parkland in the 1860s were facing hardship. By the mid–1800s, the herds of bison, once millions of head strong, were only a memory.

In 1876, the Cree signed Treaty No. 6. They ceded 309,760 square kilometres (31 million hectares or 76.5 million acres) in return for reservations, annual cash payments and the promise of agricultural tools. Four bands settled around Hobbema. The Blackfoot Confederacy followed in 1877 with Treaty No. 7, giving up 128,000 square kilometres (12.8 million hectares or 31.6 million acres) in exchange for reservations east of Calgary and west and south of Fort Macleod.

THE GAETZ FAMILY

Settlers came to Central Alberta for many reasons: to better their lives, to own their own land, to make their fortune. The Reverend Leonard Gaetz, a Methodist clergyman, moved to the south bank of the Red Deer River for health reasons and to act as the local agent for the Saskatchewan Land and Homestead Company. Gaetz undertook his new job with zeal, and became an energetic promoter of the Red Deer area. He arrived with a pregnant wife and 10 children and settled on a farm in what is now downtown Red Deer. In short order, he bought a store at the Crossing for his son Raymond, while he settled into the business of farming.

Raymond Gaetz prospered at the Crossing, trading with native peoples and providing goods for settlers. When the railway surveyed track through Red Deer, he promptly moved his store to the hamlet. He was well liked and respected in the community. Gaetz lent his energies to establishing a school and public library, and served as the first mayor.

The Crossing

Wolf Crossing, McDougall Crossing or just the Crossing—all refer to a shallow ford on the Red Deer River west of the city. Low banks and a wide, shallow sandstone shelf provided safe footing for bison, native peoples, Red River carts, freight wagons and farm wagons. The safest ford for 60 to 80 kilometres in either direction, the Crossing became the focus of a settlement as early as 1872. The trail eventually linking Calgary and Edmonton crossed the river here and freighters made a good business transporting supplies and people between the two settlements.

By the early 1880s, 30 settlers had begun farming in the area. The future looked bright and soon the Crossing boasted a ferry service, store, post office and stopping house. But in 1885, news of a massacre at Duck Lake in Saskatchewan panicked the local population. The white settlers were a minority in a largely native and Métis land. Some of the settlers took flight, packing their few belongings and fleeing to the safety of Fort Calgary. The rapidly organized Alberta Field Force quickly marched northward to calm settlers and to protect them from any insurgence. As the Field Force passed through settlements, units were left behind for their defence. Lieutenant J. E. Bédard Normandeau, with seven non–commissioned officers and twelve privates, remained at the Crossing, where they fortified the stopping house and waited for something to happen.

Nothing ever did. Within two months of their arrival, the unit was sent north to rejoin the Alberta Field Force; the Rebellion was over. The fort became the barracks for the North West Mounted Police in 1886.

Immigration

Good farmland in the United States was becoming scarce. News of the rich farmland and the Canadian government's generous homesteading policy began to draw more and more settlers to Central Alberta. The first were citizens of Ontario and Nova Scotia, generally Methodists, who had learned of the available land from the Saskatchewan Land and Homestead Company. The brainchild of the Reverend Alexander Sutherland, the SLHC was granted title to 46,080 hectares (180 sections) of land around the Crossing. The Reverend Leonard Gaetz moved to the area in 1884 to act as the SLHC's representative.

Britons were the desired settlers in Canada, where a *British is best* attitude prevailed. However, the United Kingdom could not provide the numbers required to people the west and Canada soon turned its gaze southward. After all, most Americans had British ancestry and could bring money, machinery and a knowledge of farming to the new country. Many settled in the Lacombe area where land was still free, choosing not to buy farmland from the SLHC.

Parade on Ross Street, 1907.

More settlers poured in. Icelanders settled near Markerville, Danes near Dickson and Finns near Sylvan Lake and Eckville. Most Scandinavians moved to Canada after first settling in the United States. Other immigrants, from France, Belgium, the Netherlands, Germany, Estonia, Lithuania and eastern Europe also settled in Central Alberta, but in much smaller numbers.

Red Deer Settlement

Rumours of a railway from Calgary to Edmonton had buoyed the spirits of many Crossing residents. Imagine their surprise when the C and E Railway was not directed through their settlement, but several kilometres to the east across lands owned by the Reverend Leonard Gaetz. The decision about where to locate the railway was precipitated by Gaetz's offer of land for a town if the railway crossed his property. A shrewd business man, Gaetz had already built a sawmill nearby, anticipating the influx of settlers needing construction materials for homes and commercial properties. The construction of the railway in 1890 created a rush to buy lots in the new town. By the end of 1891, numerous houses, stores and a hotel lined the streets. The North West Mounted Police moved to the town from the Crossing in 1893. Soon, the Crossing had all but disappeared. Even the fort was dismantled and moved to a nearby farm. Red Deer grew quickly, earning designation as a hamlet in 1894, a village

SALADS

Lobster   Lettuce   Tomato

FISH

Boiled B. C. Salmon, Mayonnaise Sauce   Claret

ENTREES

Orange Fritters, Wine Sauce   Tenderloin Steak, Mushroom Sauce

Breaded Lamb Chops, Green Peas   Veal and Ham Pie

BOILED

Boiled Pickled Tongue   Boiled Ham, Mustard Sauce

ROASTS

Roast Turkey, Cranberry Sauce   Brown Sherry

Domestic Chicken, Dressing   Roast Loin of Beef, Horseradish Sauce

Roast Veal and Dressing

Menu from "Capital" Banquet, held as part of Red Deer's bid to become the provincial capital of Alberta, April 17, 1906.

one year later and a town in 1901. A creamery opened, as did two brickyards and a grain elevator. By 1906 Red Deer boasted an opera house, a hospital, court house, two newspapers, several churches, a sawmill, quarry and its own telephone system.

In 1905, Alberta became a province. Red Deer townspeople wined and dined politicians and offered Michener Hill as the site for the provincial legislature, but to no avail. The capital was awarded to Edmonton, a much larger centre, and home to many of the most powerful politicians. The provincial crest, however, was designed by a local woman, Barbara George.

The ensuing years followed a pattern of boom and bust. Red

Sir Wilfrid Laurier driving the first spike for Alberta Central Railway, August 1910.

45

Deer became a divisional point for the Canadian Pacific Railway. The Alberta Central Railway, hotly pursued by the Canadian Northern Railway in a race to reach the coal fields of Nordegg, began to lay track in 1910. The town prospered and soon established itself as a transportation and agriculture service centre.

But another bust followed the boom and when Red Deer became a city in 1913, few people seemed to notice.

The Great War

When the Great War broke out in 1914, Red Deer showed its patriotic fervour. British descendants and immigrants enlisted to form the 35th Central Alberta Horse Regiment, 31st Battalion, C Squadron of the 12th Canadian Mounted Rifles, 89th Battalion, 187th Battalion, 191st Battalion and the 50th Battalion. The army used the city's fairgrounds for training new recruits.

While the war raged in Europe other battles were fought in Central Alberta. The Women's Christian Temperance Union lobbied for prohibition until the province was declared *dry* in 1915. Irene Parlby of Alix, one of the Famous Five, raised her voice for women's equality.

After a few prosperous years, farmers were again faced with a recession.

The Nordegg Coal Fields

In 1907, Martin Nordegg, a German engineer, prospected for coal in the foothills. He staked several coal fields about 100 kilometres west of Rocky Mountain House for the German Development Company. A few years later, Brazeau Collieries Ltd. formed to extract the sub–bituminous coal for powering steam locomotives. Production peaked at 500,000 tons of coal in one year in 1923.

Beginning in 1937, the coal was mixed with pitch, a tar–like substance, and formed into briquettes for easier handling. By the 1940s, Nordegg had become the largest coal briquette manufacturer in Canada. The future seemed bright for the coal industry, until major gas and oil discoveries were made at Leduc and Turner Valley. Diesel replaced coal and the colliery lost its market. The mine closed in 1955.

Nordegg designed a mine town, carefully modelled after Montreal's Mount Royal, which he located near the mine site. The town housed over 2,500 people during the boom years. Some of these buildings, including the briquetting plant, still stand and are currently being restored.

There's MORE HEAT in

BRAZEAU NON-CLINKERING BRIQUETTES

IRENE PARLBY

In league with the other members of the Famous Five, Nellie McClung, Emily Murphy, Louise McKinney and Henrietta Muir Edwards, Irene Parlby fought for legal recognition of women as 'persons'. In 1913 she helped start what was to be the first women's local of the United Farmers of Alberta. When this group became involved in provincial politics in 1921, Parlby became the first woman cabinet minister in Alberta and the second in the British Empire. She was best known for her efforts to improve the health and education of rural residents as well as the status of women and children.

Crop prices dropped. Drought cut yields. Rural Alberta was in dire straits. The farmers decided to take matters into their own hands.

The United Farmers of Alberta became the governing party in provincial politics and the voice of rural Alberta in 1921. They encouraged the organization of co–operatives and pools. In 1923 the Alberta Wheat Pool formed, then the Co–operative Marketing Association and the Central Alberta Dairy Pool the following year. The pools and co–operatives gave farmers the strength of numbers to pursue higher prices and new markets for their grain, eggs and milk. Prosperity was on the comeback— at least until 1929.

The Great Depression set in and once again agricultural products fell dramatically in price and unemployment raged. Governments stepped in to provide employment through relief projects and to stave off the starvation of an entire population. During this time, Red Deer's court house was built and a road pushed through forests and muskegs to Nordegg. The Depression ended with the outbreak of the Second World War.

Men from Central Alberta were recruited to artillery and tank battalions. The federal government chose Red Deer as the site of a Royal Canadian Army Service Corps training centre. Construction of the camp began in 1940. Camp A–20 stretched from the corner of 55th Street and 45th Avenue to the Gaetz Lakes Sanctuary, and housed more than 1,000 soldiers at a time. Pilots trained at the new airport started at Penhold during the '30s. Flying personnel from across Canada, Great Britain,

12th Canadian Mounted Rifles leaving Red Deer, 1915.

Australia and New Zealand arrived for training under the British Commonwealth Air Training Plan. Later, the base became the No. 2 Manning Depot for the RCAF. Recruits from across the country took their first training here in flight and communications before being reassigned to other training centres.

Central Alberta Today

Since the end of the war in 1945, Red Deer and surrounding towns have continued to prosper and the population numbers to climb. While agriculture and food processing are still important industries, oil and gas exploration and extraction have played an even greater role in the area's economy. Tourism is also becoming increasingly important in the region as recreational lakes, special events like the Red Deer International Air Show and winterfests, and a variety of attractions and recreational opportunities bring more and more people to the area. Located within the city limits is Waskasoo Park. Its many natural areas appeal to hikers, birdwatchers, photographers and campers.

A greater awareness of heritage and culture has also occurred. Numerous older buildings have received provincial historic designation, while others have been saved from demolition and restored by individuals and groups.

Residents and visitors to Red Deer have the opportunity to take part in many different sports. Ball fields, soccer fields, tennis courts, swimming pools, skating rinks and indoor facilities cater to both individuals and teams. The paved and shale trail system in Waskasoo Park is well used by cyclists, joggers, strollers and dog walkers. There is fishing in the river, at Bower Ponds and at Heritage Ranch, and canoeists can put in at Fort Normandeau, Great Chief Park, McKenzie Trail, Three Mile Bend or River Bend. Cross–country ski trails are groomed in many parts of the park system and alpine skiers can fill a day or more at the Canyon Ski Area nearby.

Arts are alive in Red Deer as well. International, national and regional performers are showcased at the Centrium and at the Red Deer College Arts Centre. Displays of amateur and professional works can be seen at the Community Arts Centre, the Red Deer and District Museum, the Old Red Deer Court House, the Cronquist Cultural Heritage Centre, Kerry Wood Nature Centre and in local galleries. Stroll the grounds of the Red Deer College to see student and professional sculptures, then step into the Arts Centre to admire the fabric art mural that won a national art competition and was inspired by an aerial photograph of the Red Deer area. The Arts Centre itself, designed by architect Arthur Erickson, is also worth a look.

The Centrium.

Red Deer is only the beginning of an adventure in time, nature, sport and art. There are many other places to visit nearby. Take a look in the *More to Explore* section of this book for more ideas and fun!

Exploring Central Alberta's Parkland

Waskasoo Park

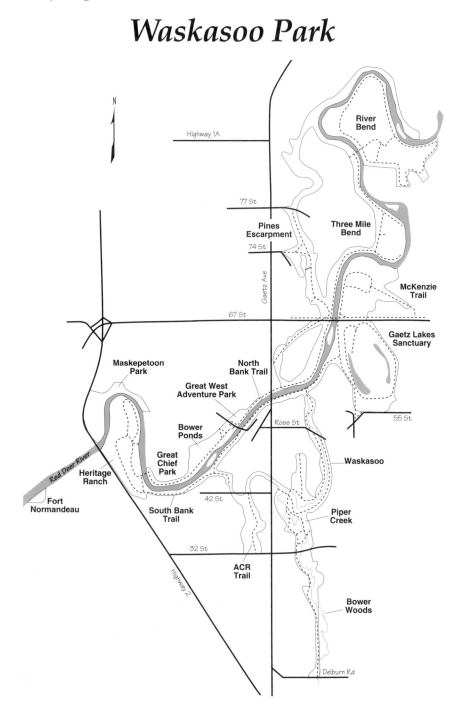

Fort Normandeau

Access: 32 Avenue west beyond Highway 2 and follow the signs
Facilities: interpretive centre, washrooms, picnic area, canoe launch, reconstructed fort, native teepee, gift shop
Environment: aspen and balsam poplar forest, riverine
Common Plants: aspen poplar, balsam poplar, chokecherry, saskatoon, beaked hazelnut, willows, wild rose, snowberry, bracted honeysuckle, pea vine, northern bedstraw, white geranium, wild clematis, red–osier dogwood
Common Animals: mule deer, coyote, red fox, beaver, muskrat, woodpeckers, common merganser, mallard, great blue heron, swallows, warblers
Special Features: reconstructed fort, special events, audiovisual presentation

Fort Normandeau marks the site of the first permanent settlement in this area. The Crossing grew at the traditional ford of the Red Deer River where a wide bench of sandstone and shallow water made for easy crossing most of the year. Both bison and people moved across the river here, and eventually the route was used by missionaries, freighters, the army and settlers.

Addison MacPherson was probably the first non–native person to live at the Crossing. A prospector, buffalo hunter, trader and freighter, MacPherson built a log shack here around 1870. He operated a freight

Fort Normandeau.

line between the railway at Calgary and Edmonton, carrying goods in wooden Red River carts pulled by oxen and driven by experienced Métis freighters. The goods were transported to the Crossing, warehoused there until everything had arrived, then transported the final leg of the journey to Edmonton.

WHEELS ON THE PRAIRIES

The Red River cart was a purely prairie invention. It was built of local wood held together by rawhide. This simple construction made the cart lightweight, buoyant in river water and easy to repair. It was pulled by oxen or horses, but its most distinguishing feature was its sound: the screeching of its unlubricated axles allowed the cart to be heard before it was seen. Grease attracted dust and dirt and quickly wore out the cart's axles. The squeal was a lesser evil.

While Red River carts were used to freight goods and supplies, 'mud wagons' also carried people. These open, horse–drawn coaches were not the most comfortable vehicles, but they could carry two passengers surrounded by bags of mail and express goods. They were built low to the ground so they would not overturn easily, and when the wagons bogged down in mud, they were easily disassembled then put back together on dry ground. This feature was more than essential on the Calgary—Edmonton Trail, which was little more than a trail winding across the parkland and prairie, through depressions that filled with water in the spring.

Other conveyances were used as well, including sleighs during the winter and, once the road improved, covered stagecoaches pulled by four horses. Most people travelled by horseback since a trip by stage from Calgary to Red Deer cost a hefty $2.50 one way.

Stagecoach on Calgary-Edmonton Trail, 1880s.

When MacPherson settled at the Crossing, he had few white neighbours. In an area now encompassing Alberta and Saskatchewan, there lived about 20,000 natives, fewer than 10,000 Métis and 1,600 whites. Of the latter, most were in Saskatchewan, at fur trading posts and their settlements or along the national border. Traveller William F. Butler wrote in 1872 that "One may wander 500 miles in a direct line without ever seeing a human being, or an animal larger than a wolf."

Stopping houses sprang up along the freighting routes to serve the men who otherwise spent nights sleeping under a cart in the open. The stopping houses were roughly constructed, usually one-room affairs with sod roofs and hand–hewn floors. Bunks hung from the walls and those arriving late slept on the floor. Breakfast was included in the price: sow–belly pork often on the green side, bread and strong black tea. The meal was welcomed and some of the loneliness of the trail dispelled in the companionship of other freighters.

M. P. Collins opened a stopping house at the Crossing in 1883. Collins sold his establishment to another freighter, Thomas Lennie. A few years later, Mary Lennie helped Raymond Gaetz with his store by teaching him Cree and trading with the native people who came to barter furs.

MacPherson and the Lennies were joined by other adventurous souls. In 1883, G. C. King of Calgary hired Robert McClellan to build the Crossing's first store. McClellan proceeded to erect a two–storey hotel next door. This palatial building, at least by local standards, had dove–tailed corners, a staircase leading to the upper sleeping quarters, a proper stove to supply heat and a shake roof. It was a far cry from the other stopping houses and it sheltered freighters, government census takers, clergymen and surveyors.

By 1885, the Crossing was a busy place. Mail service and stagecoaches regularly delivered letters and passengers. Sage Bannerman's ferry kept goods and travellers relatively dry while crossing the Red Deer River. White settlers outnumbered both Métis and native peoples.

The Spruces, the only remaining stopping house, now rests, fully restored, in the Pioneer Village Museum in Innisfail.

Homesteaders were turning meadows into vegetable gardens and grain fields. Others had set down roots near the Crossing and a second settlement, called Red Deer, was established downstream.

The routine of making a living on the frontier was shattered when news of a fierce battle at Duck Lake, Saskatchewan reached the settlers. Métis and native people had fought and killed several white settlers and North West Mounted Police officers. Fearing that a similar uprising might take place in Red Deer, the terrified settlers fled to Calgary and did not return until the threat of an uprising had been quelled.

For many years, native and Métis people had watched as the bison numbers dwindled and the trickle of white settlers turned into a flood. Although treaties had been signed and the natives were assured of government rations while making the transition from buffalo hunter to farmer, the supplies came only sporadically and in insufficient quantity. Surveyors were crossing their lands, taking bearings and making notes. The Métis had bitter memories of their displacement from lands in Manitoba by incoming settlers. Desperate and afraid, the Métis, led by Louis Riel, tried to seize hostages at Duck Lake as a bargaining tool in proposed talks with the federal government. The attackers met resistance and in the ensuing fight killed 12 people.

The Northwest or Riel Rebellion had begun. Other Riel followers raided settlements at Frog Lake, Saddle Lake and Lac La Biche. Locally settlers felt threatened but no clash occurred.

The rebellion sent tremors of fear across the prairies. A home guard was hastily organized and a message sent to the Minister of Militia and Defence requesting troops. The Alberta Field Force was recruited under the command of Major–General Thomas Bland Strange. The Field Force included 35 cowboys forming the Alberta Mounted Rifles, the 60–man Steele's Mounted Scouts, the 104-strong homeguard under Major James Walker and a detachment of North West Mounted Police with their own nine pound field gun. A further 850 troops, including the 65th Battalion Mount Royal Rifles, were speeding to Calgary by train.

While the troops were training and supplies and transportation being arranged, Father Albert Lacombe and the Reverend John McDougall were travelling among their native congregations preaching peace. Father Constantine Scollen had already calmed the local natives.

The first column of the Field Force departed Calgary on April 20, 1885, shortly after a heavy snowfall. They arrived at the Crossing tired, cold and foot–sore. The river was high and hampered their efforts to cross. The second column arrived a few days later and built a ferry to transport their supplies and soldiers across the raging waters. All proceeded uneventfully until the guide rope broke and the ferry, loaded with men and the field gun, was swept five kilometres downstream. The gun was disassembled, hauled up the steep riverbank and returned to the Crossing. The troops reached Edmonton on May 5 to ensure the safety of the settlers before continuing on to Batoche.

A small group of men, led by Lieutenant J. E. Bédard Normandeau, remained at the Crossing for the protection of local settlers. They commandeered McClellan's hotel and set to fortifying the structure. Over the next six weeks, they built a second wall filled in with river clay, dug a well, erected a two-and-a-half metre-thick palisade, excavated a moat and raised three bastions from which to watch the countryside for

The Crossing 1887.

attackers. Their work was completed three weeks after Louis Riel surrendered at Batoche.

While Normandeau and his troops saw no action, their presence was a comfort to the settlers and a source of income. The soldiers, who were paid 50 cents a day, were tired of hardtack, canned beef and tea, and readily bought fresh bread for a dollar a loaf, milk at a dollar a quart, eggs at 25 cents each and homemade beer for 25 cents a glass. Other settlers sold the detachment hay for their horses, drugs and other supplies and services. Only McClellan fared poorly since the conversion of his hotel into a garrison had not been approved by the government and therefore a complete investigation had to take place before his claim for $1,645.75 in damages could be considered.

Life returned to normal in the communities at the Crossing and Red Deer. McClellan's hotel, its appearance much changed, kept its military role by housing the local detachment of the North West Mounted Police. A non–commissioned officer (NCO) and five constables ensured that law and order was maintained along the Red Deer River and within a radius of about 65 kilometres. As well as mediating altercations between settlers, the police searched wagons for illicit alcohol and prosecuted those who set fires or left camp fires burning. A fire sweeping through the parkland where there were no fire–fighting crews or equipment was a frightening prospect. It was the constable's duty to put out any fire he found. After the arrival of the Calgary and Edmonton Railway, the police officer was also expected to greet all trains.

For the last few years of the Crossing's existence, the NCO and four constables were almost the only residents, the fifth officer having been posted in Red Deer. The arrival of the railway in 1891, and its construction at Red Deer instead of the Crossing, created a rapid

---

IT'S A POLICE OFFICER'S LIFE!

A posting at the Crossing must have been dreary indeed. The occasional report of a horse–thief or an assault must have caused great excitement. The officers' daily journals include entries such as 'scrubbing barracks' or 'brushing horses' more often than descriptions of thrilling chases or brazen criminal acts. Searching passing travellers for illicit liquor was routine as, it seems, was the disposal of the offensive fluid, according to a correspondent for the Regina Leader in 1889:

"During the last month or two most of the members of the NWMP here (at Fort Normandeau) have been affected in a peculiar way, which some of the settlers attribute to whiskey. The doctor's aid has not been needed for recovery, and possibly a short interview with a superior officer may stop for a time a recurrence of the symptom."

The report created a scandal and an official inquiry into conditions at the Crossing was called. The newspaper later retracted its story.

migration of Crossing residents to the new townsite. The police finally followed two years later, but only after using the fort's log palisade for firewood.

After the NWMP abandoned McClellan's hotel, the fort stood empty. In 1899, after removing the upper storey, the fort was moved to a nearby farm to serve as a farm building.

Across the river another story was unfolding. With the Rebellion out of the way, the Dominion government still had to deal with the native people. Acting upon the request of the Methodist Church, the government funded an Indian Industrial School opposite the Crossing. The school welcomed young natives and tried to assimilate them into white society. Part of the day was spent in school work; after reading, 'riting and 'rithmetic came pig and dairy farming, crop planting and harvesting. While the boys learned the essentials of farming, blacksmithing and carpentry, the girls mastered the domestic arts of cooking, laundering and ironing. By 1899, 90 students were enrolled, yet many native families were still loathe to break up the family and send their children to a residential school far from the reserve. The principal felt this ambivalence about the school keenly and suggested that enrolment be mandatory. This suggestion was never put into force. The school survived until 1919, then became a training centre for veterans wanting to settle in the area. None of the original structures remain.

In the mid–'30s, the Central Alberta Pioneers and Oldtimers Association initiated the reconstruction of Fort Normandeau in an effort to commemorate the Crossing settlement. The logs were recovered and the structure rebuilt, minus its second floor and bastions, near the original site of the fort. The Association was unable to maintain the site over the years and it passed to the provincial government, which established a campground on the site.

In 1974 as an RCMP Centennial Celebration project, the Central Alberta Pioneers and Oldtimers Association joined with the City of Red Deer, the Royal Canadian Mounted Police and a local service club to reconstruct the original fort with bastions and a palisade. The reconstruction was based on an inaccurate 1886 drawing of the fort. A few of the original squared logs were salvaged and can be seen in the gable ends. One section on display shows names carved during idle hours by men stationed at Fort Normandeau.

Fort Normandeau was redeveloped, then opened in 1986 as part of Waskasoo Park. An interpretive centre, built into the hillside overlooking the original river crossing, houses an audiovisual program and exhibits about the history of the Crossing and its people—white, native and Métis.

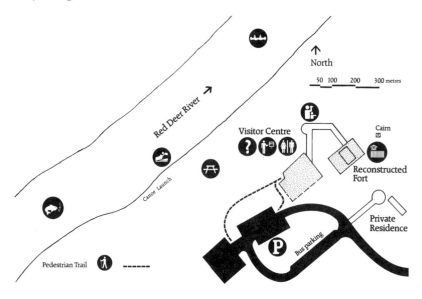

Fort Normandeau offers a step into the past. You can tour the reconstructed fort and try your hand at typical fort activities such as rope making, sock washing, planting of a heritage garden, poultry feeding and cooking on a wood stove. Check your aim with real, horse–used shoes at the horseshoe pit, or if you are part of a group, try a tug of war or other historic game. Special events are held throughout the summer, including re-enactments of battles and military drill by the 65th Mount Royal Rifles, Addison MacPherson Days (highlighting Scottish heritage and occasionally, highland games), garden planting, and Métis and native heritage celebrations. The fort, interpretive centre and gift shop are open Victoria Day weekend to Labour Day; the grounds are open May 1 to mid–October. Special programs for school and youth groups can be arranged by calling the fort at 403-347–7550 or the Interpretive Program Office at 403-346–2010.

Heritage Ranch

Access: Heritage Ranch is located at the western edge of Red Deer at the west end of 43rd Street (Cronquist Drive). It can be reached by vehicle by following the signs north from 32 Street, or from Highway 2 northbound. Southbound vehicles on Highway 2 take the 32 Street exit then follow Heritage Ranch signs. Cyclists and pedestrians can reach Heritage Ranch on the South Bank Trail or from Bower Ponds on the North Bank Trail.

Facilities: At Heritage Ranch: visitor information centre and snack bar, gift shop, washrooms, equestrian centre (trail rides, hay rides, pony rides), picnic tables, playing field, bicycle trails, viewing tower, hiking trails, cross–country equestrian course, fishing pond, group picnic shelters, playground, future site of Alberta Sports Hall of Fame and Museum

Environment: spruce woods, aspen forest, riverine forest, meadow

Common Plants: white spruce, balsam and aspen poplar, red–osier dogwood, saskatoon, chokecherry, wolf willow, bedstraw, sarsaparilla, wild rose, purple clematis, horsetail, marsh skullcap, evening primrose

Common Animals: Richardson's ground squirrel, coyote, red fox, red squirrel, mule deer, snowshoe hare, beaver, muskrat, occasionally moose, ruffed grouse, red–tailed hawk, great horned owl, bank swallow, blue jay, magpie, common flicker, belted kingfisher, Franklin's gull, American goldfinch, sparrows and warblers

Special Features: view of Maskepetoon cliffs, Lower Heritage Ranch wildlife area, old spruce forest, year-round Visitor Information Centre, equestrian opportunities, special events

Heritage Ranch is aptly named—the area has been used as a ranch for over a century. Raymond Gaetz was the first owner, staking his home quarter section in 1885 then adding a second quarter in 1889. He operated a store at Red Deer Crossing from 1884 until 1891 when he moved his operation to the new hamlet of Red Deer. Gaetz was active in the new settlement, becoming the first mayor in 1901. He was instrumental in establishing the first school, located not far from Heritage Ranch.

The Gaetz farm later became part of the Valley Ranche (see Great Chief Park—Bower Ponds). Eventually, the land was bought by William Sebastian Hoopfer. Hoopfer moved to eastern Alberta from North Dakota in 1906. The farming was good until the Great Depression and its accompanying droughts killed Hoopfer's crops and livelihood. The family decided to move to greener pastures. They dismantled their farm buildings and loaded box cars with the lumber, a few head of cattle and a horse, and set out for Red Deer. Once they arrived, they set to clearing land and rebuilding their farm. The first few years were tough and the family made do with a granary for living quarters. Selling firewood from their own woods helped to make ends meet.

After the Second World War, the Hoopfers began selling the abundant sand and gravel found near the river. The pits left from this mining can still be seen along the walking trails in Lower Heritage Ranch. One of these old pits, after some reclamation work, was converted into a popular fishing pond stocked with rainbow trout. In 1975, the Government of Alberta purchased the ranch for $220,000, then sold it to the City of Red Deer in 1982 for incorporation within the new Waskasoo Park.

Gateway to Waskasoo Park

From Heritage Ranch, bike trails and walking paths reach into Waskasoo Park. Stop here for maps and firsthand information on the park trails and local and regional attractions, events and accommodation. The Visitor Information Centre is open year-round and friendly staff will help you plan an hour, an afternoon or a few days in Red Deer. Children enjoy exploring Mickey's Activity Corner in the main building. Washrooms and a concession with a fire pit and tables can also be found here.

Just outside the main building is a viewing tower. It sways as you climb to the top! The view, however, is worth the few minutes of climbing.

Just beyond the tower is the horse stable and corrals. Meet some huge draft horses ready to pull you along on a hay ride or get friendly with one of the calm saddle horses. Pony rides are available for little tykes. Sometimes other farm animals may be visiting the ranch for you to pet or just admire.

A ball diamond and picnic area are yours to use as well.

Park trails wind through the entire ranch area. The valley floor can be reached by either a set of stairs dropping through a cool spruce forest or by following the paved bicycle path across an old pasture and down

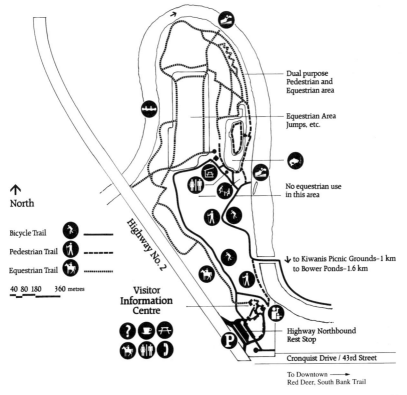

North

Bicycle Trail

Pedestrian Trail

Equestrian Trail

40 80 180 360 metres

Visitor Information Centre

Highway No. 2

Dual purpose Pedestrian and Equestrian area

Equestrian Area Jumps, etc.

No equestrian use in this area

↓ to Kiwanis Picnic Grounds–1 km
to Bower Ponds–1.6 km

Highway Northbound Rest Stop

Cronquist Drive / 43rd Street

To Downtown ⟶
Red Deer, South Bank Trail

through an aspen forest. A gravel trail leads from the stairs to the bicycle trail and the pedestrian bridge over the Red Deer River—this is the shortest route to the river from the ranch buildings.

The trails can be travelled on foot, by bicycle, on cross–country skis, on a hay ride or on horseback. Bring your own horse or join ranch wranglers for a ride into the wilder sections of Lower Heritage Ranch.

Families and children enjoy the trip to Lower Heritage Ranch. A bicycle ride or a half–hour walk from the upper parking lot takes you to a picnic area with a playground and fishing pond. A picnic shelter near the pond can be reserved for family gatherings, birthday parties or an office get–together by calling 403-342–6100.

Watch For Wildlife

Lower Heritage Ranch is a haven for wildlife and aside from the Gaetz Lakes Sanctuary, it is the wildest region of the park. Narrow walking and equestrian trails are worth investigating and lead to glades thick with wildflowers and open forest filled with bird song. The mixture of forest, river edge and open grasslands attracts mule deer, coyote and moose.

WOODWORKERS

Dead and dying trees are a fact of life for a healthy forest. The city has a policy of leaving dead and dying trees standing in natural area parks such as Heritage Ranch, unless they are a danger to people or facilities. A dead tree takes on a new life as a source of food and shelter for a number of animals. Along with ants, beetles and other bugs, old trees are a great place to look for woodpeckers. Five woodpeckers are common in Central Alberta: common flickers plus downy, hairy, three–toed and pileated woodpeckers. Listen for the woodpeckers throughout the year, but especially in the spring. During the mating season, woodpeckers seek out hollow trees to act as drums: their amplified hammering resonates through the forest to announce the bird's territory and to attract females.

The most common woodpeckers in Waskasoo Park are the downy (left) and the larger hairy (right) woodpeckers.

Watch for the calling cards of these birds as you walk along forest paths: a pile of bark flakes at the base of a spruce marks the visit of a three–toed woodpecker; a rectangular hole shows the dining area of a pileated woodpecker. Round holes are the front doors to homes of flickers, downy and hairy woodpeckers. All these birds search for insects found under the bark or within the punky wood.

How Much Wood Could a Woodchuck Chuck...

You may want to recite this childhood ditty as you scan the high banks of Maskepetoon Park overlooking the river, but you probably won't get an answer. The few woodchucks or groundhogs that inhabit this bit of wilderness are pretty shy. Your best bet is to sit by the river on a warm day and look for these overgrown ground squirrels sunning themselves near the cliff edge.

Groundhogs are low, stocky animals about the size of a fat rabbit. They are built for digging; each groundhog has a burrow with up to 25 metres of tunnels often running five metres deep. Several entrances give the animal extra protection when danger, a coyote, fox or unleashed dog, approaches.

Groundhogs don't tolerate close neighbours except during the mating season. The young remain with the mother until late summer before setting off to establish territories of their own. Territories are fiercely protected and a fight can leave the combatants with deep wounds from their large, powerful teeth. Most of the summer, groundhogs can be seen quietly going about their own affairs, grazing near their burrow, digging a deeper den and preparing for winter hibernation.

Red squirrels inhabit the spruce forest, arguing indignantly with any trespasser, large or small. Woodpeckers are active throughout the area; listen for their hammering on dead and dying trees. Look for browse marks, twigs clipped by deer, moose and snowshoe hare, along the river. Mallards and mergansers rest on the water and beaver can often be seen on the banks felling trees or feeding on willows. Above you rise the Maskepetoon cliffs.

The Maskepetoon Cliffs

Trails lead to the river edge and the towering Maskepetoon cliffs. The last 60 million years of geological history are written on the cliff face. At river level, a layer of sandstone reflects earlier times when Central Alberta was warm, and shallow swamps filled up with river–borne sand. Above the rock lie pre–glacial gravels, a thick layer of sand and rock worn smooth and round by rushing rivers. These rivers were rapidly eroding the

Rocky Mountains rising ponderously in the west and carrying their booty of quartzite, sandstone and limestone to the flatter lands far from the mountain front. These waterways snaked over the plains for about 54 million years. The pre–glacial gravels are blanketed by a hodge–podge of rock, gravel, sand, silt, coal and petrified wood dropped by passing glaciers. Unlike the gravel, the rocks are more angular, still showing the rough edges that were once attached to Rocky Mountain cliffs or Canadian Shield bedrock. This glacial till is covered, in turn, by a thin sheet of sand, clay and silt—the remains of an ancient lakebed once filled by glacial Lake Red Deer. Capping the cliffs is the topsoil formed in the last 10,000 years or so.

The cliffs are the handiwork of the Red Deer River. As the topsoil was building at the top, the river was slowly chipping away at the sandstone and gravel at the bottom. Periodically, the cliff face collapses from the undercutting. The river quietly sweeps the debris downstream, then resumes its assault on the cliff. The river deposits debris from its excavation at a bend in the river farther downstream. There, as it did in Lower Heritage Ranch, the river gradually builds up the bank on the inside of the curve and forms a point bar.

The changes in the riverbanks can best be seen by canoe. Launch your craft at Fort Normandeau, then paddle, or float, past cliffs, point bars, exposures of sandstone, islands, gentle rapids and the bustle of the city.

BEAVER TROUBLE

Beaver are common throughout Central Alberta. They make their homes in ponds, lakes, and along creeks and rivers. They eat the tender inner bark of trees and bushes, and build domed lodges of the leftover sticks cemented with mud, or excavate long burrows into riverbanks for homes. Their dams cause flooding and high water along creeks. To produce their feats of engineering they need trees—lots of trees.

Trees are often planted to beautify and to provide shade. To prevent valuable trees in residential districts or in ornamental parks from falling victim to the beaver's ever–growing teeth, Red Deer's Parks Department wraps wire mesh around particularly tasty trees. Both beaver–chewed trees and protected ones can be seen around Bower Ponds and in other areas of the park, especially in the Sanctuary and near Waskasoo and Piper creeks.

Occasionally, the high water behind a beaver dam may endanger bridge footings or other structures. When this happens, the dam is destroyed and the beaver trapped. In most cases, though, the city has a hands–off policy and beavers are allowed to do what beavers do best: alter the landscape and create new habitat for themselves and other animals.

Maskepetoon Park

Access: from Kerry Wood Drive, at the fork in the road continue west on the gravel road
Facilities: none
Environment: tamarack swamp, white spruce forest, wetland
Common Plants: tamarack, white spruce, willow, red–osier dogwood, sedges
Common Animals: red squirrel, groundhog, mule deer, moose, coyote, least weasel, chickadees, blue jay, nuthatches, brown creeper, kinglets
Special Features: tamarack swamp, gray jay, Tennessee warbler

The wildlands of Maskepetoon Park are bounded by the Red Deer River on the south and east, Highway 2 on the west and Kerry Wood Drive to the north. The park stretches along the high cliffs on the north side of the river to include a sliver of grassland before dropping down the slope into the cool, moist forest of white spruce and the park's only tamarack swamp. At river level, the park includes small wetlands rich in both plants and animals. Future plans include formal walking trails, viewpoints and interpretive signage when housing is developed north of Kerry Wood Drive.

A short, rough trail skirts the high riverbank. An early summer walk among the aspen poplars and grassy meadows is a feast for the eye and

MASKEPETOON—PEACEMAKER

Maskepetoon was a powerful Plains Cree chief in the mid–1800s. He frequently travelled through this area, using the ford at the Crossing to enter into Blackfoot territory. In his youth, these forays into enemy lands were in search of scalps; later they were missions of peace.

In the mid–1840s, Maskepetoon began to question the need for violence and warfare between the two enemy nations. After a period of meditation and prayer in the solitude of the foothills, Maskepetoon undertook a lifelong commitment to making peace with the Blackfoot.

For many years, the Cree and the Blackfoot lived in relative peace. Maskepetoon was felled by a Blackfoot arrow in 1869 as he was approaching a camp to negotiate a peace pact.

the nose. A profusion of wildflowers grows among the trees, including shrubs such as wild rose and red–osier dogwood and forbs like blue clematis, false Solomon's seal, bracted honeysuckle, western Canada violet, harebells and white geranium. Wild rose and wolf willow scent the air with heady perfume. Come back a month later, and the saskatoons, then the chokecherries, will be ripe for picking.

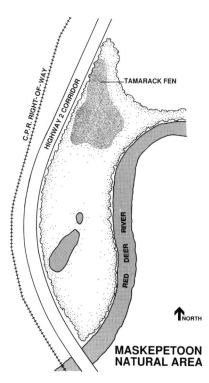

MASKEPETOON NATURAL AREA

South Bank Trail

Access: The South Bank Trail stretches from Heritage Ranch with access at a variety of points including 43 Street, 60 Avenue and 56 Avenue; the Taylor, CPR, Gaetz Avenue and 67 Street bridges; 48A Avenue and 45 Avenue.

Facilities: shelter at Gaetz Avenue, washrooms available at Kerry Wood Nature Centre

Environment: spruce woods, aspen forest, riverine forest, meadow

Common Plants: white spruce, balsam and aspen poplar, red–osier dogwood, saskatoon, chokecherry, wolf willow, bedstraw, sarsaparilla, wild rose, purple clematis, horsetail, marsh skullcap, evening primrose

Common Animals: Richardson's ground squirrel, red squirrel, snowshoe hare, beaver, muskrat, bank swallow, blue jay, magpie, common flicker, belted kingfisher, Franklin's gull, American goldfinch, sparrows and warblers

Special Features: historic sandstone quarry, Janet Cook Arbour, Historic Walking Tour

The South Bank Trail is very popular with cyclists and joggers. It skirts the Riverview Park acreages along Cronquist Drive (43 Avenue) before turning north to reach the riverbank. The trail turns north near the location of Red Deer's first school, marked by a cairn, then follows the riverbank to the east.

The Crossing School

A school was of the utmost importance to local settlers. But where to put it? There were the McClellan children at the Crossing to the west and the Gaetz children in the hamlet of Red Deer. A compromise was reached and a school was built in 1887 midway between them on an unused road allowance. The Crossing School opened with an enrolment of seven—five Gaetzes and two McClellans—taught by William Vrooman. He was replaced the following spring by Nova Scotian George Wilbert Smith. The log school was open for classes through the spring, summer and fall and closed during the winter. In 1892 the Crossing School closed and the students, now numbering 22, moved to a new school in Red Deer. A replica of the log school now stands in Heritage Square next to the Red Deer and District Museum.

Red Deer's Bridges

The trail continues beside the river under Taylor Bridge, named for Ethel Taylor—the first woman elected to Red Deer's city council—and past the city's water treatment plant. A steel train bridge spans the river and provides walkers and cyclists access to North Red Deer. This bridge is the second one at this spot. The first was built in 1890–91 by the Calgary and Edmonton Railway. Just a flag stop, the Red Deer station—a box car set next to the tracks—only saw a train once a week. In 1907, Red Deer became a divisional point for the Canadian Pacific Railway and the old wooden bridge was replaced by one made of steel. This bridge continued to be used until 1991 when the CPR moved its rails to the west of the city.

This historic landmark was scheduled to be demolished once the trains stopped running. The Northside Community Association, assisted by the Normandeau Cultural and Natural History Society, spearheaded a Save the Bridge campaign. Through their tireless efforts, donations from individuals and volunteer labour from the United Brotherhood of Carpenters and Joiners Local 2410 were marshalled. The bridge was upgraded to continue to serve as an important link between North and South Red Deer. Today, the bridge is a starting point for the North Red Deer historical walking tour, a one-and-a-half hour stroll past old homes, commercial buildings, a convent and a sawmill site. Or, head south on the road to Gaetz Avenue and Fiesta Plaza at 55 Street to start the Gaetz Park historical walking tour. This one hour walk passes by the historic homes of many of Red Deer's most influential citizens: Reverend Leonard Gaetz, one of Red Deer's first settlers and promoters; William Addison Moore, the originator of the city's electrical system; and F. W. Galbraith, newspaper publisher and first mayor of the city.

The South Bank Trail passes under a second bridge, the Gaetz Avenue traffic bridge and enters Gaetz Park. To the south are the Janet Cook Arbour and the Harold Snell Gardens.

Red Deer's new railroad bridge, 1909.

69

The Reinholt Quarry

Below the trail, identified by an interpretive sign, lies Red Deer's first sandstone quarry. Henry Reinholt began supplying local builders with the stone in 1891. St. Luke's Anglican Church, the Greene Block (5001 Ross Street) and many house foundations and lintels were built with this grey rock. One beautifully carved stone found its way to the Red Deer Cemetery, where it marks the grave of the

Reinholt family. The quarry, while finding a local market, was not a major industry. By 1914 other construction materials and techniques were favoured and the quarry closed.

FLOWERS FOR THE CITY

Janet Cook was a teacher of French, an independent and proper lady. When she died in 1982, she left her money to 32 charities and $33,000 to the city. There was a purpose for the gift: to enhance Gaetz Park. An arbour with benches and fragrant flowers was built at the west end of the park.

At the top of the hill near the strip mall, colourful flower beds catch the eye of passing motorists. These gardens honour Dr. Harold J. Snell, one of Red Deer's earliest residents. Snell was a community–minded man. When he wasn't working at his optometry practice, he served Red Deer's citizens as mayor, alderman and chairman of various local groups. Snell enjoyed working with plants and was well known for his spectacular flower beds. This colourful corner of the city was dedicated to Dr. Snell in 1967.

An afternoon jaunt through Gaetz Park, 1912.

Gaetz Park is one of the oldest green spaces in the city and is considered the nucleus of the park system. In 1909, Halley Hamilton Gaetz, the son of Reverend and Mrs. Leonard Gaetz, donated 3.6 hectares (nine acres) of land to the city in memory of his deceased parents. The memorial was fitting: the elder Gaetzes' home overlooked this stretch of riverbank and they no doubt enjoyed its beauty.

The Red Deer Advocate noted in 1909 that "...it will be a matter of great gratification to the citizens that the handsome gift from Mr. H. H. Gaetz to the Town of the land along the river...will give the Council a splendid start to beautify that section of the river front, and to make it a convenient park resort for the citizens. No park is complete without a considerable body of water and few parks could be more happily situated in that respect than Gaetz Park."

The gift of a park rather than a monument or building was typical of Red Deer residents' fondness for parks and wild spaces. Few cities can boast of largely untouched river sides forming a continuous green belt that can be used by both people and wildlife to move up and down the river valley. Gaetz Park shelters many birds among both the river edge willows and the old spruce and balsam poplars. People living above the park are used to seeing snowshoe hare tracks patterning the snow in their backyards or catching a glimpse of a red fox slipping away into the bush.

At the mouth of Waskasoo Creek, near the eastern end of Gaetz Park, wooden footings are all that is left of the Canadian Northern Railway bridge. The CNR ran a line from Red Deer to the Brazeau coal fields near Nordegg. Trains approached the bridge on a 30 metre-long wooden trestle, crossed the river in four spans then continued northward on another trestle. The bridge was built of Howe trusses—a technique often used when skilled carpenters were not available at the bridge construction site. The bridge was prefabricated elsewhere, dismantled, then reconstructed on site.

The wooden piers were subjected to attacks by floods of Waskasoo Creek and the river, and by ice jams in the spring. After the bridge was destroyed and rebuilt repeatedly, the CNR gave up. The bridge was abandoned in 1941 after a final timber–crushing ice jam.

The South Bank Trail crosses Waskasoo Creek and passes the junction with the Devonian Trails that follow the creek to the south edge of the city. The South Bank Trail crosses 45th Avenue and enters the grounds of River Glen School operated by the county of Red Deer for rural students. A short walk brings you past the Gaetz Lakes Sanctuary, the Kerry Wood Nature Centre and to McKenzie Trail Recreation Area.

ACR Trail

Access: from 43rd Street just west of the hospital, or from 32nd Street by Taylor Drive
Facilities: picnic shelter, washrooms
Environment: riverine, disturbed
Common Plants: balsam poplar, willows, red–osier dogwood, cattail, Canada thistle, sweet clover, alfalfa
Common Animals: beaver, woodpeckers
Special Features: beaver activity

The ACR Trail parallels Waskasoo Creek and Taylor Drive from 43 Street to the Red Deer College grounds. Although wildland on either side of the creek has largely disappeared due to road and housing construction, the creek itself is quite interesting.

Waskasoo Creek originates near Penhold. It catches water from farm land, city lawns and parking lots. It reacts quickly to heavy rainfalls or snowmelts and has been known to cause serious flooding along its course. When swollen with stormwater, it flushes stagnant pools and rearranges the beaver dams and log jams that interrupt its freedom.

In spite of the urban sprawl that has engulfed its banks, the creek is still a highway for wildlife between the farmlands to the south and the Red

Deer River to the north. Beaver especially use this corridor when migrating from their place of birth to an uninhabited stretch of water. Signs of beaver are everywhere: chewed down trees, new and old dams spanning the creek, ramshackled lodges and caved in bank burrows.

Plants, too, use this corridor. Disturbed land and farm fields are seed sources for non–native plant species. Alfalfa, clover, sweet clover, sow thistle, wormwood and Canada thistle thrive along the creek banks, often growing where the land was disturbed. Some are beneficial to wildlife while others are, plain and simple, weeds.

Some of the non–native plants followed the rails into town. ACR stands for Alberta Central Railway. The ACR was incorporated in 1901 and its directors planned to build a railway right across Western Canada. The president of the company was John T. Moore, also the manager of the Saskatchewan Land and Homestead Company (SLHC). The railway would open up lands owned by the SLHC and make land more saleable. For a price, no doubt.

Nothing happened for eight years. Finally, the federal government offered a subsidy to the company for the construction of the line from Red Deer to Rocky Mountain House. The result was incredible: brush was cleared, grading begun and in just over a year, the residents of Red Deer gathered to watch Prime Minister Sir Wilfrid Laurier drive the first spike.

The crash of the mallet was like a starter's pistol; the race was on! Coal had been discovered in the foothills west of Rocky Mountain House and a German firm was beginning to build a mining town—Nordegg. The

FRANCIS, RED DEER'S FAVOURITE PIG

Sometimes natural corridors are used by non–native visitors. Such was the case with Red Deer's most famous pig.

In the fall of 1990, Francis was bound for the sausage machine when he escaped into the freedom of the park. He eluded farmers and park employees, trackers and animal fanciers for several months, and elicited sympathy and offers of adoption from across the country. Finally, as winter was turning down the thermometer, Francis was found. During the capture, a poorly aimed tranquilizer dart pierced the spunky porker's paunch, speeding his journey to pig paradise.

Painted by David Plumtree.

ACR geared up to be the first railway to the coal fields. But the Canadian Northern Railway had also set its sights on servicing the mine. The two railways worked feverishly, often side by side, to gain a lead in the westward push. Workers, not ignorant of the competition, held out for higher wages. Material costs soared. The competing workers brawled, the lawyers haggled over rights–of–way and the railway managers coped with terrible headaches. In 1911 the race was over: the ACR gave up at Rocky Mountain House. The CNR continued pushing westward but at a less frantic pace.

Less than 80 years later, this link with Western Alberta has all but disappeared. All that is left are concrete bridge piers near 43rd Street, portions of the rail grade and a 633 metre-long (2,112 foot) trestle bridge over the Red Deer River. The trestle was completed in 1912 after almost two years of construction. Fifteen towers support the metal bridge. During its construction, the project engineer sent a strong swimmer across the swollen Red Deer River with a rope to fix to the other bank. This was the start of a 148 metre (445 foot) suspension bridge needed to move men and supplies across the river. The trestle bridge can be seen best from a canoe.

The ACR Trail ends at the Red Deer College grounds. The college's trails take over to lead hikers into the sandhills south of the buildings. This area, south of the college to Highway 2, is comprised of dunes formed from sand blown off the shores of glacial Lake Red Deer over 12,000 years ago. White spruce, balsam and aspen poplar and a host of shrubs and wildflowers conceal the dunes. Trails through this area wind among creekside forests and hilltop spruce woods.

Bower Ponds and Great Chief Park

Access: from Kerry Wood Drive; by bicycle or foot from North Bank Trail; from Taylor Bridge

Facilities

Bower Ponds: pavilion with washrooms, snack bar and sports rentals (canoes, paddle boats, skates, bicycles, fishing tackle, cross–country skis); fishing pond, tobogganing hill, skating pond (lit at night), paved trails

Great Chief Park: playing fields, Kiwanis Picnic Grounds, playground, canoe launch, pitch and putt, washrooms

Environment: poplar forest, riverine, river, disturbed/man–made

Common Plants: willows, red–osier dogwood, wild rose, cattails, aspen and balsam poplar, exotic/non–native trees and shrubs

Common Animals: common merganser, mallard, common tern, belted kingfisher, ring–billed gulls, mountain whitefish, northern pike, walleye, suckers, exotic/domestic waterfowl

Special Features: Cronquist Cultural Heritage Centre with tea room, gallery and gift shop, Canada Day Festival (July 1), open air concerts, former mill ponds converted to a variety of recreational uses, playing fields

The Trail West

From Bower Ponds, the trail system stretches past Great Chief Park and the private Red Deer Golf and Country Club west toward Heritage Ranch.

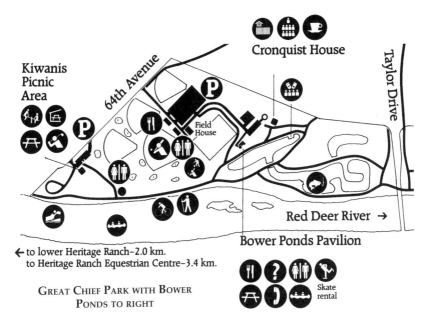

Cronquist House

Kiwanis Picnic Area

64th Avenue

Taylor Drive

Field House

Red Deer River →

Bower Ponds Pavilion

← to lower Heritage Ranch–2.0 km.
to Heritage Ranch Equestrian Centre–3.4 km.

GREAT CHIEF PARK WITH BOWER
PONDS TO RIGHT

Skate rental

The golf club area was formerly the Valley Ranche. Homesteaded by Walter and Alfred Reade in 1885, the land made a respectable farm, only to burn to the ground two years later. Although they rebuilt with the help of their neighbours, they only stayed a few years in the valley. In 1889, brothers George and Francis Wilkins, with their mother and sister, took possession of the ranch. While George followed the lure of gold to the Cariboo, Francis, or Ted as he was known, remained to become a citizen of some stature in Red Deer as the elected representative to the Territorial Assembly. The brothers eventually formed a partnership and built a hydroelectric plant and dam on the Blindman River at Burbank. They hadn't counted on the low water in the river during the summer and their business never really succeeded.

The Kiwanis Picnic Grounds are at the end of Fountain Drive near the river. After a picnic at one of the many open air tables or in the picnic shelter, the whole family can have fun tossing horseshoes at the horseshoe pit, climbing and swinging in the playground, strolling along the river, testing their skill at a nine-hole pitch and putt course or taking in a game at Great Chief Park.

Continuing west past the golf course, the trail crosses the river to lower Heritage Ranch. This stretch of trail is called the Peace Mile, so designated by city council in 1993. Upper Heritage Ranch is three kilometres away.

MURDERER ON THE LOOSE!

The Valley Ranche was the backdrop for Red Deer's only Wild West gunfight. In 1892, murderer Ole Mickleson was pursued by a civilian posse into the valley. Mickleson had bludgeoned a travelling companion to death near Edmonton and had stolen his money, a whopping $317. He quickly travelled south, following the railway. A farmer near Red Deer spotted him, rounded up some friends and set off in pursuit. Bullets hailed the woods where the posse cornered the desperado. When Mickleson ran toward the ranch house where Mrs. Wilkins and her daughter were hiding, one of the posse, William Bell, shot him. Bell was arrested and charged with manslaughter, but the jury found him innocent after deliberating for a whole minute.

The Trail East

Great Chief Park and Bower Ponds are the premier recreation areas of Waskasoo Park. The range of activities offered here appeals to families, groups and sports teams. Teams play slowpitch, fastball, baseball, soccer, rugby and football on the diamonds and sportsfields. Tournaments often take place here as well. The fields are lit for evening games. To find out who is playing today, or to book a ball diamond or sportsfield, call 403-342–6100.

Great Chief Park was named after the Great Chief—Maskepetoon, an illustrious Cree warrior and peacemaker (*see Maskepetoon Park*). Maskepetoon was well known throughout Central and Southern Alberta for his efforts to forge a lasting peace between the Cree and Blackfoot peoples.

Bower Ponds is named after Hugh Bower, who strongly supported the proposal of the Red Deer Fish and Game Association to turn this industrial site into a natural area with trout ponds. Bower saw his dream fulfilled when his initial generous donation was matched by others; today people enjoy boating and fishing here all summer. Paddle boats and canoes can be rented at the pavilion, or you can bring your own. Fishermen young and old can try their luck, courtesy of the fish stocking program funded by the Red Deer Fish and Game Association. Remember though, if you're over 16, you need an Alberta fishing licence.

In winter, the ponds freeze and are flooded and maintained for skaters. A roaring fire in the centre of the main pond welcomes budding figure skaters and young hockey superstars. What better way to get some winter exercise! A cup of hot chocolate, available next to the skate and ski rental in the pavilion, warms you up from the inside. Summer's grassy slopes turn into an exciting tobogganing hill, and trails for cross–country skiing radiate from this meeting place.

The North Bank Trail follows the river past Great Chief Park and Bower Ponds and under the Taylor Bridge to Great West Adventure Park.

Cronquist House

A quieter time can be spent at the Cronquist Cultural Heritage Centre. The house has a tea room—call 403-346–0055 ahead to check for times. Upstairs, ethnic arts and crafts are displayed, sold in the gift shop and taught in classes. The centre can be booked for meetings and functions. Most of the building can be visited; the creaking of the wooden floors makes it easy to imagine that the ghost of Cronquist House is watching over your shoulder!

The centre is housed in a beautiful three–storey brick house that was moved to this site in 1976 from a spot across the river. Emmanuel Petterson Cronquist and his family, Swedish immigrants, moved to Red Deer in 1903 to farm. Cronquist hired an architect to build his dream home, using local brick from the Piper Creek brickyard (*see Waskasoo/ Piper Creek Trails/Bower Woods*). The 325 square metre (3,500 square foot) house was completed in 1912 and was the home of Cronquist family members until the farm was sold for the West Park Estates housing development in the mid-seventies. The developer offered the house to the Red Deer International Folk Festival Society, which raised the funds needed to move the house across the river. Cronquist House is now fully restored and was designated a Municipal Historic Resource in 1982, the first in Alberta.

The Great West Lumber Company, Millpond, 1912.

The Lumber Story

The land occupied by Great Chief Park, Bower Ponds and Great West Adventure Park has an interesting story of its own. A growing, thriving community needs land, good water ... and lumber. The Reverend Gaetz brought a small sawmill into the area in the late 1800s, in competition with the McKenzies who were also intent on supplying settlers with planks. But it wasn't until 1905 that a large sawmill was established in Red Deer. George H. Bawtinheimer bought the needed equipment from the Alberta Lumber Company and began to operate, producing 25,000 to 40,000 board feet of lumber per day. In 1906, he sold his holdings to the Great West Lumber Company, which expanded the mill. The mill itself was located on the hill overlooking the mill ponds, now Bower Ponds.

The sawmill was one of the city's largest industries, employing 100 people in a town of 2,000. Logs were cut near Sundre, floated down the Red Deer, then directed by a chain strung across the river into a sluiceway. The sluiceway fed into mill ponds that extended from the Bower Ponds pavilion to Great West Adventure Park. As logs were needed, they would be dragged from the ponds onto an inclined ramp and into the mill. When heading toward Heritage Ranch the trail passes over the sluiceway, now overgrown with vegetation.

The company prospered and expanded its operation in 1911 and 1912. Its production peaked the following year with an output of 180,000 board feet in a day. Good fortune was only temporary. An accident at the sawmill and losses of logs during flooding in 1915 crippled the company. Finally, a drop in construction during the war years silenced its saws in 1916, putting almost 100 men out of work.

Great West Adventure Park, North Bank Trail, Lions Campground

Access: from Kerry Wood Drive near Taylor Drive, by bicycle or foot from North Bank Trail or South Bank Trail via Taylor Bridge

Facilities:

Great West Adventure Park: BMX track, washrooms, boat launch, paved trail

Lions Campground: 127-stall full service campground, washrooms with showers and laundry facilities, interpretive amphitheatre programs, playground, dump station, North Bank Trail

Environment: disturbed/man–made, mature balsam poplar and white spruce forests, riverine

Common Plants: balsam poplar, white spruce, aspen poplar, chokecherry, saskatoon, wild rose, beaked hazelnut, snowberry, willow, red–osier dogwood, asters, false Solomon's seal, bedstraw, lungwort, harebell, sarsaparilla

Common Animals: red squirrel, least chipmunk, beaver, magpie, blue jay, black–capped and boreal chickadees, robin, sparrows, belted kingfisher, red fox; bald eagle, osprey, gulls, ducks, and great blue heron along the river

Special Features: BMX track, old Canadian Pacific Railway bridge, access to North Red Deer, boat launch

Great West Adventure Park

Once the site of a thriving sawmill operation, Great West Adventure Park is the site of a bicycle motocross (BMX) track with challenging moguls, camelbacks and a tunnel. Local, regional and national championships are held here periodically and, most days, a few aspiring competitors are trying out the course. (*See Bower Ponds and Great Chief Park.*)

to Lions Campground-1.5 km →

The North Bank Trail

The North Bank Trail follows the river past Great West Adventure Park, giving views both up and down stream. Often kingfisher can be seen sitting on an overhead wire or patrolling the river for small fish. Ring–billed gull loaf on the gravel islands that appear in the river in the summer. Jet boats scream along this stretch of river, practising for races or just for the sheer joy of it. The water is shallow and inviting, but swimming is not recommended near the water intakes for the water treatment plant!

The North Bank Trail intersects the right-of-way at the old Canadian Pacific Railway bridge and skirts North Red Deer (*see South Bank Trail*). This bridge was used until 1991 by freight trains. When the rail line was relocated west of the city, the bridge was slated for demolition. Now the bridge is the starting point for a one hour-long historical walking tour of North Red Deer.

North Red Deer developed as a community distinct from Red Deer. Its predominantly Catholic and largely French population settled near the mission founded by the Fathers of Sainte Marie of Tinchebray from Normandy, France. Religious lines were drawn along the river: most settlers in South Red Deer were Protestant. North Red Deer was incorporated as a village in 1911 and soon elected its first council. The priority for the council? To improve the wooden sidewalks and roads that connected the residents with the school, the sawmill, the tannery and other businesses. North Red Deer became part of Red Deer in 1947.

The North Bank Trail continues east under the traffic bridges and along the perimeter of Lions Campground. Watch for the scars on the river side of older trees along the trail. Before the construction of the Dickson Dam and the resulting lower water levels in the spring, ice jams were frequent. The pans of ice heaved onto one another and choked the river from one side of the valley to the other. The ice scoured the riverbanks and crashed into trees high above water level, removing patches of bark and scarring the trees.

Lions Campground

The original Lions Campground was built by the Lions Club in 1966 as a Canadian Centennial project. The city later took over the campground and expanded the facility. The west end of the campground caters to tenters and small trailers not needing hookups. It is nestled into a mature forest of white spruce and balsam poplar. Saskatoon, chokecherry, hazelnut, red–osier dogwood, willows, wild rose and high–bush cranberry encircle the individual campsites. The entrance to the campground, and the full hookups area, is the site of an old cement plant. Some of the rubble from the plant has been bulldozed into a hill where parks staff have planted a variety of domestic flowering plants. Watch for wild red foxes in this area. Interpretive programs are offered regularly during the summer on the other side of 'Mt. Rubble' and are open to everyone.

The trail curves with the river and heads northward toward Three Mile Bend. This stretch of trail passes through thick willow tangle. A few quiet minutes with a pair of binoculars and a bird guide should deliver a number of different warbler species. Red–winged blackbird are also common, and

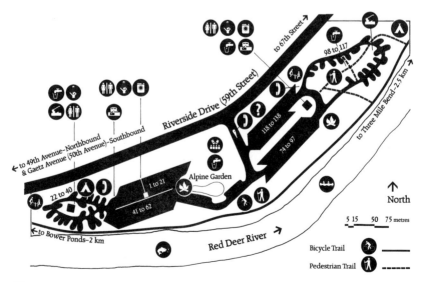

Lions Campground.

several duck species as well as ring–billed gull and Canada goose make their homes on the island across from the Kerry Wood Nature Centre.

WILLOW GALLS

Many of the willows lining the trail between Lions Campground and 67 Street have strange growths near the tips of their branches. Some look like pine cones, while others look like withered brown roses. These are galls, the product of a tiny insect called a midge. Midges lay eggs at the tips of the willow's branches. Something—either a chemical secreted by the midge or an injury to the bark—causes the branch to grow abnormally. The egg hatches and the midge  larva burrows into the gall where it spends the winter. In the spring, it bores a hole in the wall of its chamber and flies away.

During the winter, the petals or scales of the galls harbour many other insects. Watch for chickadees and other insect eaters probing the galls in winter in search of a little hibernating protein.

The trail passes under the 67th Street bridge and continues on to Three Mile Bend. Above and to the west is the Pines Escarpment. It can be accessed from this point by following 67th Street to a trail that heads toward the escarpment. The escarpment can also be reached from Parsons Close, Piper Drive and Page Avenue in the Pines.

Fish Tales

What fish live in the Red Deer River? Alberta Fish and Wildlife decided to find out. Starting in 1991, fisheries technicians began studying the river between the Dickson Dam and the Joffre Bridge and its inhabitants. In shallow water, fish were shocked with an electrical current. While they were stunned, the fish could be closely examined and counted. In deeper water, the researchers went snorkelling! A few fish were caught and tagged with radio transmitters. These fish were tracked by boat and by plane and their movements were recorded.

Some changes have occurred since the dam was built. Mountain whitefish are still the most common swimmers in this stretch of river, but few spawn. Their relative, the lake whitefish, is increasing in numbers but is still fairly uncommon. Other fish found in low numbers are northern pike, perch, walleye and mooneye.

The mooneye was once quite common; now few are found. The goldeye population, however, has exploded. This cold water–loving fish has similar habits to the mooneye and has moved into its vacated niche.

Brown trout were planted in the river and found it to their liking. More nests, or redds, have been found in each year of the study. Brown trout have been found spawning in the Medicine and Blindman rivers. In a few years, the population may be large enough to support sport fishing.

What other changes are in store for the river and its fish? Besides the dam, there are other factors that affect fish populations and the health of a river: the amount of rainfall and snowmelt, when it falls, whether spring water flows can flush the river and scour the riverbed, pollution from agricultural herbicides and pesticides, as well as urban pollutants such as oils and other wastes and sport fishing pressure.

While we can't change the effects of the dam or influence rainfall and snowmelt, we can do something about pollutants and sport fishing. Oil, paint, turpentine and other toxic liquids can be disposed of during annual toxic round–ups hosted by the city. Why not start or join a community clean up of the river or creeks? Fishermen can help, too, by practising catch and release. Perhaps the mooneye will never come back, but we can all make the river a healthier place for other fish, and people, too.

Waskasoo, Piper Creek, Bower Woods Trails

Access: This trail system runs from the river to the Delburne Road and can be accessed from neighbourhoods all along its length. See map.

Facilities: playgrounds, washrooms, picnic areas, recreation centre, museums, skating oval, tobogganing hill, curling rink, arena, tennis court, Participark

Environment: riverine, aspen forest, balsam forest, spruce woods, maintained lawns

Common Plants: cattails, willow, red–osier dogwood, alder, aspen poplar, balsam poplar, white spruce, asters, wild clematis, goldenrod, false Solomon's seal, wild sarsaparilla, wild rose, highbush cranberry, raspberry, horsetail, one–sided wintergreen, bishop's cap

Common Animals: red squirrel, red fox, coyote, mule deer, beaver, muskrat, black–billed magpie, American crow, waxwings, nuthatches, chickadees, redpolls, ruffed grouse

Special Features: Heritage Square, Recreation Centre, Red Deer and District Museum and Archives, Rotary Picnic Park, Parkvale Walking Tour, Kin Kanyon

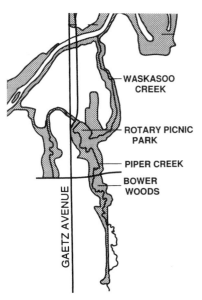

WASKASOO CREEK

ROTARY PICNIC PARK

PIPER CREEK

BOWER WOODS

GAETZ AVENUE

This section of Waskasoo Park, also known as the Devonian Trail System, has everything one could want in a park along its length. Groomed lawns, bicycle and hiking trails, picnic areas, playgrounds, wild areas, heritage sites and recreation areas are easily accessible from both sides of Waskasoo and Piper creeks.

Starting from the north end, the trail heads south from the South Bank Trail at Gaetz Park. It winds among huge balsam and spruce trees before entering Galbraith Park on 55th Street. This little park, squeezed between Waskasoo Creek, houses and a busy street, commemorates Red Deer's first mayor. Francis W. Galbraith moved to Red Deer in 1905 to become editor of the newspaper he purchased, the Red Deer Advocate. He became active in municipal politics and was elected mayor in 1912. When Red Deer became incorporated as a city the following year, Galbraith earned the distinction of being the first mayor of the City of Red Deer.

The Galbraith home is located nearby at 5810 – 45 Avenue and should be viewed with the Gaetz Park Historical Walking Tour in hand.

Park users must cross busy 55th Street at the street light to proceed south on the trail. The path skirts the banks of Waskasoo Creek, a drab little stream for much of the year. Its looks are deceiving, however. Northern pike and some suckers seek out Waskasoo Creek to spawn in the spring. The yellowish pike eggs stay glued to plants until they hatch. Suckers spread their eggs over gravel beds, where the eggs hatch in about two weeks. After spawning, the fish return to the deeper, cooler water of the Red Deer River.

Spring can be a dangerous time along the creek, for animals and people alike. As spring thaws turn the countryside to mud and water, the creek swells with the runoff. Rotting ice may look strong and stable, but is likely to collapse when stepped upon. The waters rise each spring for a week or so, scouring the streambed and destroying any beaver dams barring their rush to the river.

Beaver and muskrat make their homes along the entire length of this waterway. Occasionally, a dam spans the creek, producing a deep, wide pool upstream, the perfect home for a beaver. Bank burrows, where a

MICKEY THE BEAVER

One of Red Deer's best known and best loved residents was a beaver named Mickey. The injured beaver kit was brought to the Forbes household by a passerby. Wally and Mary Forbes doctored the kit's wounds while their daughter, Doris, became his closest friend. Mickey was devoted to Doris, spending time at her bedside when she was sick, following her on walks along Waskasoo Creek, swimming with her in the creek and in a backyard pond and pining after her whenever she was away.

The little beaver soon grew to be a big beaver, weighing over 35 kilograms when he died at the age of nine years. In those nine years he entertained over 20,000 visitors from neighbours to European tourists. No matter the time of day (beaver are most active between dusk and dawn), Mickey always seemed

Mickey and best friend Doris Forbes.

pleased to be stroked, picked up and offered treats of fresh peas, carrots and fruit. During the war, the Forbes agreed to display Mickey at the fair to raise money for food parcels for soldiers overseas.

Mickey's story is best told by author Kerry Wood in his book *Mickey the Beaver and Other Stories*. Once known to so many, Mickey still lives in the hearts of Red Deer residents as a city mascot.

beaver has excavated a tunnel and den well into the streambank, are more common here than domed stick lodges. The soft earth and the fairly stable banks lend themselves to construction of underground dwellings. The muskrat follows suit, either digging a bank burrow, building a lodge out of mud and vegetation, or simply making a creekside nest for the summer.

Between 53rd and Ross Street lie Stephenson and Coronation parks, a grassy expanse with clusters of stately old spruce trees. The open spaces are perfect for a game of pickup football or frisbee, or to relax on one of the benches with a good book and watch the people going by. These parks, like Barrett Park farther south, are a pleasant spot for a stroll.

Stephenson Park honours two brothers who arrived in Red Deer near the turn of the century from Ontario and became respected citizens. William James Stephenson settled here in 1911 and joined the Gaetz–Cornett Drug and Book Company as a partner. He was very active in the community, serving for many years on the school board and municipal hospital board.

Victory Park.

Albert Thorburn Stephenson arrived in Red Deer with a survey crew and stayed on to work as a teacher at the Crossing School and later became principal of the town's new school. His energies turned to municipal affairs and he served on the town council for three years before being appointed secretary–treasurer and commissioner. He administered the city's business for over 27 years, dedicating himself to the progress and beautification of Red Deer.

Coronation Park celebrates several events in the history of the British monarchy. The park was established in 1937 upon the coronation of King George VI, and five spruce trees, marked by bronze plaques, were planted. In 1953 a weeping willow was added to the park's southeast corner to commemorate Queen Elizabeth's ascension to the throne. A spruce tree, planted 25 years later, marks her Jubilee. The southeast end of Coronation Park near Ross Street is frequented on Saturdays by wedding parties for photo sessions.

Tucked into a corner of land separating Ross Street and 49th Street lies tiny Victory Park. Established to celebrate the victory of the Allies during the Second World War, it is best known for the streetscape sculpture at its heart. The artwork was commissioned in 1980 as part of Alberta's 75th anniversary and produced by Edmonton artist Dean Eilertson.

Across the street is Barrett Park, named for Robert Edward Barrett, one of Red Deer's longest serving mayors. This energetic man arrived in town in 1918. After working for a time at the Alberta Meat Market, he bought the operation and continued to operate it until 1964. In 1961 he turned his sights to city affairs and was elected to council. After four years, he moved into the position of mayor, where he remained for nine years before retiring. During his tenure, he involved himself with municipal organizations on a provincial level.

Barrett Park follows the curve of Waskasoo Creek to 48th Avenue. It skirts the old Exhibition Grounds, once the scene of large agricultural fairs. The first fair took place in 1892 with exhibits of livestock, grain, vegetables and preserves, but the venue moved every year. In 1902, the Red Deer Agricultural Society moved to the flats near Waskasoo Creek and the site became known as Alexandra Park. The fairgrounds grew in size over the years as a racetrack, an exhibits building, stables, livestock pens, a grandstand, arena and curling rink were added.

During the First World War, the buildings were turned into barracks for the Canadian soldiers in training prior to leaving for Europe. Agricultural exhibitions continued to be presented annually and were well supported, even when such fairs were cancelled in most other communities for lack of funds. The grounds were used until 1982 when the new exhibition ground, Westerner Park, was constructed at the south end of the city. Today, the curling rink and the arena remain. Now the local Farmer's Market fills the parking lot every Saturday morning from Victoria Day until Thanksgiving.

West across 48th Avenue at Rotary Picnic Park, long–time residents will tell you, was the site of an auto park. Tourists could pull in and set up a tent or spend the night in cabins while visiting Red Deer's sights. During the Depression, these cabins housed families on relief.

Barrett Park.

Library.

A few minutes walk from the park stretch the old CN rail yards, now the home of the Red Deer and District Museum and Archives, Rotary Recreation Park and Heritage Square.

The Red Deer and District Museum and Archives is the home of Red Deer's past. Preserved in documents in the archives and in artifacts in the museum, the city's and area's history is brought to life through permanent and temporary exhibits, special displays and events, and public programs. The collection includes fossils, archaeological artifacts, agricultural equipment, household furnishings, textiles, clothing, and Inuit and Indian art. Art shows are held throughout the year. The museum and its gift shop are worth a side–trip from a park visit or at another time for their own merits.

Aspelund Laft Hus.

Rotary Recreation Park is a complex of indoor and outdoor facilities. The Recreation Centre houses indoor and outdoor pools, a sauna, hot tub, offices, and meeting and craft rooms used for courses such as pottery, drawing and children's art. Outside, you can spend your time playing tennis, splashing in the wading pool or monkeying around in the playground.

Heritage Square, adjacent to the museum and the recreation centre, preserves some of Red Deer's historical structures, including the Presbyterian Church steeple, the Gaetz library, the Stevenson–Hall Block, and reconstructions of the Crossing School and a Norwegian Laft Hus. Tours of the buildings are available during the summer months, starting at the museum. The sod–roofed Laft Hus is open frequently during the summer and special arrangements to tour this traditional log house can be made by calling 403-347–2055.

The museum is also the starting point for the Parkvale and Downtown historical walking tours. A brochure for these tours can be picked up at the museum, or join an interpreter for a guided walk during the summer. The Downtown Tour is 3.9 kilometres in length and requires almost two hours to complete; the Parkvale Tour is 3.3 kilometres long and takes just over an hour.

Nearby are other historical structures, including the old Armoury (now part of the library), the Old Court House Community Arts Centre and City Hall Park. The Armoury and the Courthouse are good examples of old buildings being preserved for new uses. The Armoury became part of the Red Deer Public Library in 1994. The Old Court House houses an art gallery, coffee shop, and offices of numerous arts and cultural groups.

City Hall Park is a pleasant spot to visit during the summer when thousands of flowers in every hue and fragrance are in bloom. Intended as a picturesque courtyard surrounded by public buildings, park planners first had to remove a hill in the centre of the park. Eight hundred loads of dirt later, the park was ready for landscaping.

City Hall Park.

Real old-timers will tell you of a brickyard, the first industry in Red Deer, once located just west of this site. It closed in 1922 after operating for nearly 30 years. William Piper came west in 1891, searching for good farm land and a place to start a brickyard. He found the two requisite ingredients just the other side of Piper Mountain: clay in the west bank of Piper Creek (behind the motel) and water. While taking other work to sustain the family while the fledgling business established itself, Piper focused on building kilns and other facilities. Mechanical equipment for manufacturing the brick was added in 1899 and steam power two years later. The brickyard was producing well and employed up to 60 people. By 1914, 50,000 bricks per day were produced.

The brickyard could not compete with the brickyards in Redcliffe and Medicine Hat where fuel costs were substantially lower. Although no longer able to compete, the Piper Brickyard had contributed to the growth of Red Deer. The pale orange-coloured bricks can still be seen around town in the Cronquist House, the CPR Station and the Parsons House currently housing the Red Deer Native Friendship Society.

No old-timers still living can tell you about the use of this site thousands of years ago by nomadic buffalo hunters. Archaeological investigations at the top of Piper Mountain uncovered evidence of several campsites: fire–broken rock, charcoal, butchered animal bones and pieces of stone tools. Small groups of hunters, perhaps just family groups, spent one night, maybe two or three, camped on the hill. What they were looking for can only be guessed at—bison to hunt, berries to harvest or this may have just been a pleasant rest stop on a longer journey. We will never know for sure.

No people were around at all when the huge metasequoia, now a grey, fossilized stump near the parking lot of Rotary Picnic Park, sprouted, grew, died and fell into a swamp where it turned from tree to rock. Although this chunk of petrified wood was found outside of Red Deer, it is representative of the plants that thrived here when the dinosaurs were dying out.

Today, Rotary Picnic Park is one of the most popular park areas. A wonderful adventure playground built with toddlers to pre–teens in mind hums with excitement and fun during the summer. A large picnic area surrounds it with washrooms and a group picnic shelter. The shelter can be booked by calling 403-342–6100. Wood and water are available. Refreshments can often be purchased at a small stand.

Trails leaving the picnic park climb to the summit of Piper Mountain and loop through the woods and along the creek. Although located in downtown Red Deer, Rotary Picnic Park is at the mouth of the Piper Creek Valley, a reasonably wild area. Birdwatchers will find a multitude of warblers nesting in the willows lining the creek. Woodpeckers can be heard pounding their hard beaks against the softer wood of dead and decaying balsam poplars in their search for ants and grubs or nesting sites. Listen as you walk for rustlings in the underbrush—you have a chance of seeing a chipmunk, a porcupine or even a skunk.

A walking trail follows the west side of the Piper Creek Valley, while a paved bicycle trail follows the east side. The two trails meet at Kin Kanyon. Along the bike trail you can stop for a fitness break at the Participark. Different activities test your strength and endurance.

Kin Kanyon is another area of the park where the whole family can have fun. A playground, picnic site and wading pool, as well as open grassy areas, are well used by people who live nearby. In winter, tobogganing is the sport of choice, but watch out for the trees at the side and bottom of the run!

The trail passes under 32nd Street and enters Bower Woods. This next stretch is like hiking in a mountain forest: white spruce tower over you and filter out most of the traffic noise. You can imagine yourself far away from the city, surrounded by wilderness. The creek meanders nearby and side trails lead past small sloughs with beaver dams and lodges. The fragrance of the spruce on a hot summer's day mingles with the perfume of wild roses.

The Bower Woods were once part of a large farm belonging to the Bower family. Piece by piece, sections of the homestead were carved off, some for city parkland, most for residential and commercial development. Above the trail to the west are the remains of the Bower farm, now the Sunnybrook Farm Agricultural Interpretive Centre. The Red Deer and District Museum Society is operating a museum focusing on the role of the family farm in Central Alberta.

In too short a distance, the trail climbs out of the valley near Bower Place Mall. Cyclists and walkers can continue south along the utility corridor to the Delburne Road and the Westerner Grounds.

A MOOSE ON THE LOOSE!

Where in Red Deer can you find moose? Try Kin Kanyon and the Bower Woods. But why are there moose in the City of Red Deer?

Piper Creek starts in the sloughs and fields south and east of Red Deer. Creek and river valleys are often used as highways by wildlife, especially where surrounding forests have been felled and turned into agricultural or developed land. Forested valleys are left wild for practical reasons: the valley walls are too steep to farm and cost more to develop, so are left for last. This is advantageous for wildlife—these valleys are natural corridors with good tree and brush cover and abundant water and food.

Moose are not uncommon in Central Alberta. They travel downstream along Piper Creek or along the Red Deer River. Eventually, some find their way into town. Moose have been sighted almost every year in the Kin Kanyon–Bower Woods area, Heritage Ranch and occasionally in the Gaetz Lakes Sanctuary.

Moose are fairly tolerant of people but if you encounter one, keep your distance. Males during the mating season, females with calves and any moose feeling stressed by the noise of cars and the presence of humans may charge without notice. The moose is swift and its hooves are sharp. Rather than hazard a close encounter of the disembowelling kind, retreat or give the animal a wide berth. Let the Kerry Wood Nature Centre or Alberta Fish and Wildlife know about your sighting.

Gaetz Lakes Sanctuary

Access: by road from 55 Street turn north on 45 Avenue; by foot or bicycle from South Bank Trail or Michener Centre

Facilities: Kerry Wood Nature Centre (KWNC), bookstore, picnic tables, water and washrooms in KWNC, handicapped accessible trail to bird blind, walking trail, observation decks, telescopes, meeting rooms

Environment: lake and marsh, aspen forest, balsam forest, spruce woods, grassland

Common Plants: cattails, willows, red–osier dogwood, chokecherry, saskatoon, aspen poplar, balsam poplar, white spruce, sarsaparilla, twinflower, wild geranium, prairie crocus, anemones, buttercups, wild clematis

Common Animals: red fox, coyote, mule deer, white-tailed deer, beaver, muskrat, woodpeckers, red squirrel, flying squirrel, Richardson's ground squirrel, goldeneye, bufflehead, Canada goose, coot, mallard, red–winged blackbird, red–tailed hawk, Bohemian waxwing, chickadees, nuthatches, blue jay, magpie

Special Features: Gaetz Lakes, Kerry Wood Nature Centre, federal migratory bird sanctuary, variety of habitats, audiovisual production

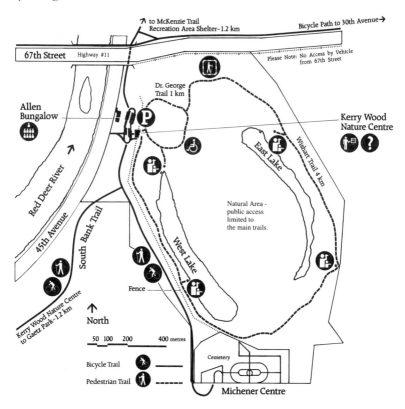

The Gaetz Lakes Sanctuary stretches from Michener Centre in the east and the cemetery to the south, to 67 Street in the north and to the school grounds and 45 Avenue to the west. Its 118 hectares (292 acres) preserve the habitats of Waskasoo Park in microcosm. Its paths wander through grasslands, poplar and spruce forests, to the edge of the West Gaetz Lake and to viewpoints where the entire valley can be surveyed. The sanctuary is a good place to start your exploration of Waskasoo Park.

In 1885, a nephew of the Reverend Leonard Gaetz arrived in Red Deer. John Jost Gaetz and his mother, Catherine, moved into a log cabin at the south end of the sanctuary in 1886. Gaetz was granted his homestead in 1890. Catherine applied for a homestead on the north end of the sanctuary the following year. The land was granted to her—an unusual decision since women were not generally given homesteads. In this case, having the Rev. Gaetz as a relative and her son able to work the land no doubt cast a favourable light on her application. According to the land agent, Mrs. Gaetz and her son belonged "to a class of settlers that are of importance to a young and growing town like Red Deer in the way of spending their money and employing labour in it."

Little of the sanctuary land could be farmed and only 11 hectares (27 acres) were ever cleared. The Gaetzes encouraged their Red Deer neighbours to enjoy the land as a park and it soon became a popular spot for picnics, skating, hiking and community get–togethers. In 1922, the Alberta Natural History Society (ANHS), a precursor of the Red Deer River Naturalists, convinced J. J. Gaetz that the area should be preserved as a bird sanctuary. He readily agreed, and under the ANHS's guidance, the land became the Red Deer Bird Sanctuary by an order–in–council of the federal government on June 27, 1924. As a federal sanctuary, no hunting, trapping or molesting of birds, or the taking of their eggs or nests were permitted within its boundaries. The ANHS became the guardian of the sanctuary and it depended upon its members, including Kerry Wood, to maintain the integrity of the sanctuary.

Although the land had been designated as a bird sanctuary, its ownership remained with the Gaetzes. After J. J. Gaetz's death in 1937, his widow sold the land to the provincial government, no strings attached. The federal designation seemed to have been forgotten as the south end became a garbage dump and a training ground for soldiers from the

THE ALBERTA NATURAL HISTORY SOCIETY

In 1906, the Alberta Natural History Society was formed in Innisfail. Within a few months, a branch of the society was established in Red Deer, and other branches in Erskine, Stettler and Medicine Hat followed.

The Alberta Natural History Club had an active membership involved in wildlife and plant inventories. Three meticulously researched booklets were produced to help amateur and professional alike in their naturalist pursuits. The greatest achievement of the ANHS, however, was the protection of the Gaetz Lakes Sanctuary. Through the society's efforts, the sanctuary was designated a Federal Migratory Bird Sanctuary. Society members, Kerry Wood and others, protected the sanctuary from every assault.

Membership in the ANHS declined over the years, and by the end of the 1930s all branches but Red Deer's had closed down. Although suffering in numbers, the local branch made up for the small membership with enthusiasm and dedication.

In the early 1970s, the society began to strengthen. Battles over the survival of the Gaetz Lakes, the development of the Dickson Dam, proposals for development in national parks and along the Eastern Slopes attracted new members with new energy.

In 1976, the Alberta Natural History Society changed its name to the Red Deer River Naturalists. Under its new name, the society became even more active in local projects such as the establishment of the Ellis Bird Farm, the development of Waskasoo Park and particularly the Kerry Wood Nature Centre, and initiating the Habitat Steward Program.

Many of Red Deer's green spaces still survive thanks to the awareness and lobbying of dedicated naturalists in the community.

nearby army camp and the lakes a duck hunters' paradise. After the war, the provincial government planned to log the escarpment; only the protests of the ANHS, Red Deer City Council, the Board of Trade, service clubs and citizens protected the land from exploitation. The upwelling of support for the sanctuary had been rekindled. When a fire threatened the wilderness area, people like Kerry Wood, Wellington Dawe and others fought the flames. In 1950, Red Deer residents pressured the provincial government to preserve the land and it was transferred to the Provincial Parks Department and designated a Provincial Wildlife Park. Once again the ANHS took charge of the maintenance and protection of the sanctuary. The provincial government provided a fence to encircle the area, while the city provided $50 and J. J. Gaetz's wife made a bequest of $1000 for improvements to the sanctuary.

Yet the sanctuary still wasn't safe. Developers unveiled plans for amusement parks, sewage lagoons and condominiums; others wanted to beautify the sanctuary by removing the underbrush to make it into a 'real' park. A highway was to run through the sanctuary. A storm sewer from Michener Centre channelled water into the East Lake, gouging a large gully into the hillside and dropping silt into the lake.

The threats to the sanctuary steeled the resolve of Red Deer's residents to protect the Gaetz Lakes Sanctuary. Students from Bob Mills' biology class at Lindsay Thurber Composite High School studied the plants, animals and waterways of the sanctuary and were the first to raise the alarm about pollutants flowing into the lakes. Members of the Alberta Natural History Society, later called the Red Deer River Naturalists, lobbied politicians to preserve the sanctuary and not permit development that threatened the integrity of the area. In 1974, City Councillor Ethel Taylor brought together representatives from several like–minded groups to form the Gaetz Lake Sanctuary Committee. Battles were fought in the political arenas, on the pages of the Red Deer Advocate and at public meetings. Through the group's efforts, a road and bridge designed to run through the middle of the sanctuary were moved to the sanctuary's north end. Finally, in 1983 the Province of Alberta sold the sanctuary land to the City of Red Deer for inclusion in Waskasoo Park.

The Waskasoo Park development was a key to the protection of the Gaetz Lakes Sanctuary. During the planning and development of the park system, citizens and interested groups were invited to express their concerns and wishes. As a result of the public input, land to the west of the sanctuary, Glenmere Farms, was acquired as a buffer between the city and the sanctuary. Fencing keeps out vehicles and ensures that this bit of wilderness remains wild.

KERRY WOOD

Edgar Allardyce 'Kerry' Wood came to Red Deer in 1918 as a youngster from New York. He spent his free moments wandering through the sanctuary, looking at and learning from the wildlife he encountered. His interminable questions were answered by friendly librarians, by the native people he met in his wanderings and by friends in the Alberta Natural History Society.

In his mid–teens, Kerry Wood decided to stay in Red Deer and make his own way as a writer while his parents moved to B.C. His first winter was a lean one, depending upon fish he could catch in the river, animals he could snare, edible wild plants and gifts from friends. The hardships of that winter, his experiences as a scout and scout leader and his many years as the volunteer warden for the Gaetz Lakes Sanctuary provided Kerry Wood with the stories that he set on paper.

Kerry Wood is still a writer, a conservationist and an educator. Although he and his wife Marjorie are now retired, his stories live on in 24 books and numerous children's readers. During his career, Kerry Wood wrote 6,200 short stories, 8,000 articles, 9,000 newspaper columns and hundreds of TV and radio programs. In 1938, Reader's Digest wrote that Kerry Wood's writing was 'a modern example of the authentic interpretation of nature through the medium of imaginative literature....' In 1990, Kerry Wood was honoured with the Order of Canada presented to him at the Kerry Wood Nature Centre by Governor–General Ray Hnatyshyn.

A few years ago, while park managers were inspecting a natural area in

Waskasoo Park, a newcomer to the city remarked that the dead trees and undergrowth should be 'cleaned up'. He soon regretted his comment as the managers lectured him on the value of dead trees to wildlife. After their outburst, they proudly stated: "Kerry Wood taught us that!"

Whether writing about David Thompson, the great mapmaker, a beaver called Mickey, Jim O'Chiese or a Scottish great horned owl, Kerry Wood mixed factual information with lots of humour and zest. Through his writings, broadcasts and personal teaching, Kerry Wood instilled a love and understanding of nature in the children and adults of Central Alberta— indeed, in people across North America.

During construction of the 67th Street bridge, the city engineers and parks staff worked with the Red Deer River Naturalists to minimize the disturbance to wildlife and the sanctuary. A berm of trees was planted to eventually give some cover for animals moving from one side of the bridge approach to the other, fencing was placed to prevent access by vehicles into the northern portion of the parkland without excluding deer, and the bridge was extended to leave space under the bridge for free movement of wildlife along the natural corridor next to the river. The Citizens Action Group for the Environment later spearheaded a campaign to plant more trees along the bridge access to provide better cover for widlife.

As part of the park development, a nature centre, named for the area's patron, Kerry Wood, trails, viewing blinds and a lookout were opened in 1986. Anyone walking, cycling or skiing through the park has an opportunity to learn more about the woods, fields and waterways around them.

Kerry Wood Nature Centre

The Nature Centre has something for everyone. Adults and families enjoy the displays explaining the natural and cultural history of Waskasoo Park. You can travel through a glacier, take a helicopter ride over the river valley, play an animal habitat game, discover how a spring works or find out about the people who saved the sanctuary for your enjoyment today. A 15–minute slide show introduces Waskasoo Park

and will give you ideas for other places to explore. The Discovery Room and a pre–schoolers' play area are full of hands–on activities that let you discover the wonders of nature at your own pace. The Marjorie Wood Gallery exhibits changing art shows and travelling exhibits on a nature theme. You can even shop at the well–stocked bookstore!

The Nature Centre offers numerous programs and courses on the natural history of Central Alberta. Teachers and youth group leaders can bring a class or group to the centre and participate in a program that fits with the curriculum and is lead by an experienced naturalist. Special events are held throughout the year. Activity packs on wildflowers, trees, snow, pond life, tracking and birds are also available for use in the park. Snowshoes can be rented, conditions permitting. Ask at the front desk for the packs and a bimonthly calendar of events. The Kerry Wood Nature Centre can be reached by phone at 403-346–2010.

Dr. George Trail

The Dr. George Trail is named after Dr. Henry George, the first president of the Alberta Natural History Society. This trail is paved for its one kilometre length, perfect for wheelchairs, strollers and small children. It loops through the aspen woods, pausing at a viewing blind over the West Gaetz Lake. The chances of seeing hairy and downy woodpeckers, nuthatches, chickadees, ruffed grouse, red–tailed hawk, a variety of waterfowl, beaver, muskrat and Richardson's ground squirrel in summer are quite good. An evening stroll may turn up a coyote or some of the resident mule deer. The trail returns to the Nature Centre through grasslands, once pasture for cattle.

Wishart Trail

The Wishart Trail begins partway along the Dr. George Trail and runs for four kilometres. This gravel trail commemorates an early resident of the area, who lived for a short while on sanctuary land but did not homestead. The trail leaves the pavement and heads into a transition belt between grassland and forest. The brush is thick here but if you look closely, you can spot animal trails piercing the thicket. These trails are especially visible in winter: snowshoe hare maintain well–packed paths to feeding areas and deer will follow specific trails over and over, especially if the snow is deep. Look for browsed branch tips at knee–height for snowshoe hare and shoulder–height for deer. Red-osier dogwood seems to be a particular favourite!

The trail continues into a spruce stand and passes the culvert home of a porcupine. This lumbering animal can move at a surprising speed and is an excellent tree climber. Should you spot it, give it room to pass by and admire the prickly back and tail from a distance. Although porcupine do not throw their quills, they do flail their tails to plant the lightly rooted, barbed quills in the nose or leg of a predator. Look for any dislodged quills on the trail after the rodent has passed.

The trail leaves the flats and climbs gradually to the Hogsback viewpoint where the panorama is breathtaking! Far below is the East Lake. A good set of eyes can spot beaver and muskrat patrolling the lake, but binoculars are a necessity to identify the variety of waterfowl that nest on the lake or rest here on their migrations north and south. The viewpoint is at treetop height, so you are eye to eye with some of the birds that are usually difficult to spot. Beyond the lake is thick forest with no access to people but a haven for wildlife. In this secluded spot, deer bear their young and coyote prowl the paths in search of mice and snowshoe hare.

As you continue along the trail, it is easy to see how the Red Deer River once swung in a big loop against the escarpment. At some point in time, the river abandoned its channel below you and moved to the west side of the valley where it flows today. It left behind an oxbow lake, divided in two by a slump or small landslide. (*See The Land Through Time p. 18.*) The two Gaetz Lakes, cut off from the river, depend on other sources for

Gaetz Lake.

water. Rainwater and snowmelt help to keep the lakes full; small creeks channel storm water from the Michener Centre grounds. In dry years, the lake levels drop and more marshland and wet meadow develop along the edges and at the north ends of the lakes. Water may be pumped into the lakes from a natural underground water source to keep them from drying up completely. In wet years, lake waters spill over the Dr. George Trail and the lower parts of the Wishart Trail in an attempt to reclaim the old riverbed.

The trail skirts the escarpment and at times, bare cliffs show the deposits of ancient glaciers and lakes. (*See The Land Through Time p. 17.*) The mud nests of cliff swallows hang from projecting ledges and holes drilled into the soft rock lead to the nests of mud dauber wasps. The sweet clover and other flowering plants provide the nectar needed by the wasps and some of the insects favoured by the swallows.

The heady perfume of wolf willow in early spring and wild rose in early summer follow you until you enter the spruce forest. Suddenly, the air becomes more moist, cooler and quieter. Sarsaparilla blankets the ground, giving way to twinflower and bishop's cap where the sun is excluded by tall evergreens. A closer look at the plants here reveals a curiosity: where else in the park can you see mountain ash, elderberry and honeysuckle? In years past, the gardeners at Michener Centre pruned and culled plantings on the centre grounds. These discards were dumped over the fence above the sanctuary. Some took root, and

continue to thrive here. While the introduction of domestic plants to a wild area can often cause the eradication of native plant species, in this case, the growth of these shrubs has provided a new and abundant source of winter berries for birds.

A set of stairs takes you farther into the spruce forest. Snow is sparse in the winter, caught by the upper tree branches. Animals move through the forest freely, but find very little reason to stay: the spruce forest is cooler in the winter and the shady floor provides little food. A common resident, though, is the red squirrel. Its chatter can be heard from the moment you enter its territory until you leave. In late summer it cuts the cones from the spruce crowns, dropping its prizes onto unwary passersby. Large heaps of cone scales mark the squirrel's midden, a larder that grows each year with both stashed cones and the leftovers from the squirrel's meals.

Before returning into the sunshine and the aspen forest, the trail crosses a small creek that issues from Rosedale Ravine, then climbs steeply to the crest of a low hill. This hill is part of the slump of land that peeled off the escarpment and slid into the lake, cutting it in two. Water collects between the slump and the valley, creating a wet area. These types of areas, as well as seepages and springs, host rare and fragile plant communities with residents like sparrow's egg orchid, round–leaved orchid, hooded ladies'–tresses, dwarf raspberry and one–flowered wintergreen. It is especially important to stay on the trail near these easily disturbed sites.

Dropping down to the edge of West Gaetz Lake, a bridge crosses a drainage channel. This is a wonderful vantage point for spotting muskrat, frogs and large water insects like water striders and beetles. Crossing the bridge, you skirt the former garbage dump and military practice grounds. This area has been reclaimed and grasses, shrubs and trees will be left to colonize the field on their own. You can already see fingers of vegetation extending from the aspen forest into the grasslands.

A raised viewing platform gives one last view of West Gaetz Lake. Slightly to the south lies a massive beaver lodge. Beaver and muskrat are often seen at dusk when they are most active. Mallard and coot are also common, but come back in the spring and fall to see flocks of swans and

THE ALLEN BUNGALOW

Across the parking lot from the Kerry Wood Nature Centre stands the Allen Bungalow. This restored historic building includes a private apartment and a meeting room that can be booked through the Nature Centre.

This large, Edwardian farmhouse was built for Archibald W. G. Allen in 1912. Allen was an Englishman who opened an accounting firm in Red Deer in 1904. He worked as an auditor for the city and for the village of North Red Deer. His skills were often in demand by community organizations such as the Agricultural Society, the Red Deer Exhibition, the Memorial Hospital Board, Red Deer Rifle Association and the Horticultural Society. During most of the First World War, Allen served in the armed forces, before returning to Red Deer for a few years. He moved to Calgary in 1920, then sold his house to the Busby family in 1931.

The house changed hands again and became part of Glenmere Farms, owned by the McCullough family. When the house and land became part of Waskasoo Park in 1985, the building was extensively renovated to its 1912 appearance. The house is now provincially designated as an Historic Resource.

Soldiers' sanitorium, Red Deer, 1922.

snow geese as they pause to rest and feed on the lake before continuing their migration.

You can migrate back to the Kerry Wood Nature Centre for a rest after your walk, to view the exhibits, visit the critters in the Discovery Room or browse through the book shop.

Two trails leave the Nature Centre for further exploration of Waskasoo Park. Following the trail to the north will take you to McKenzie Trail Recreation Area. Taking the trail to the south will bring you to a fork: the western fork joins the South Bank Trail, while the eastern or left–hand fork heads to Michener Centre. This trail is called the Michener Mile in honour of Governor–General Roland Michener, and passes Lindsay Thurber Comprehensive High School, then climbs to a viewpoint overlooking the sanctuary and 55 Street. The trail intersects the road system on the Michener Centre grounds.

The large red and white brick building, now Michener Centre's Administration Building, was built in 1913 to house the Alberta Ladies College. This non–sectarian Christian college operated by the Presbyterian Church was designed to give girls, particularly farm girls, an education. Students were accepted from eight years of age and could attend for seven years, leaving the college with a grade 11 matriculation. Courses included French, German, art, music, physical education, scripture, expression, household science and teacher training.

The costs of operating the school during the First World War proved to be a hardship and the college's Board of Directors accepted an offer of $125,000 for the building from the provincial government. The school was moved to Edmonton while the government finalized plans to use the building as the Provincial Training School for the mentally handicapped. These plans were suspended while the structure was used to care for and rehabilitate mentally ill soldiers returning from the war. By 1923, most of the soldiers had either left or been moved to the Oliver Institution in Edmonton, freeing the building for the government's intended use. Mentally handicapped people from Western Canada and the Territories were admitted to the institution, where they were cared for and, if able-bodied, trained to do housework or farm chores. For many years, the institution was largely self–sufficient, with patients maintaining extensive vegetable and flower gardens, a dairy and a cattle operation on the site. Today, only the root cellars, some of the tree plantings and the Administration Building are left from the centre's farming days. The Administration Building is a Designated Municipal Historic Resource.

The main road into Michener Centre passes by the Red Deer Cemetery. This land was once owned by the Gaetzes and a parcel of 2.25 hectares (five acres) was given to the Methodist Church by John Jost Gaetz in 1893. The land was transferred to the city in 1907. A brochure, 'The

Red Deer Cemetery, c. 1920.

Cemetery Walking Tour', is available at the Red Deer and District Museum and Archives and guided cemetery tours are regularly scheduled during the summer. Whether with a group or on your own, the cemetery is an interesting place to explore. The cemetery contains about 6,000 graves of people from all walks of life: soldiers and businessmen, clergymen and Provincial Training School residents, men and women, young and old. A walk through the cemetery is a study in art and in history.

If you follow the main road farther onto the Michener Centre grounds, you will pass by a two–storey brick and wood building. This house was built in 1918 for John Jost Gaetz and his wife, Grace. The home was the setting for many parties and was a gathering place for Gaetz's friends. The provincial government bought the home in 1938 and renovated it into a group home for boys. The house is now a Designated Municipal Historic Resource.

McKenzie Trail Recreation Area

Access: from 45 Avenue on the southeast side of the river, by bicycle on the South Bank Trail or from the North Bank Trail by crossing on the 67th Street Bridge

Facilities: three picnic areas near pond or river, group picnic shelter (for reservations call 403-342-6100), playground, washrooms, canoe launch, secluded group camping area, boardwalk, paved trails

Environment: mature balsam poplar and white spruce forests, riverine

Common Plants: balsam poplar, white spruce, aspen poplar, red-osier dogwood, willows

Common Animals: beaver, muskrat, Canada goose, snowshoe hare, red squirrel, coyote, mule deer, white-tailed deer

Special Features: reclaimed gravel pits, oldest trees in the park

The McKenzies—brothers Benjamin, David and Roderick—had an eye for opportunity. Roderick and a small group of settlers arrived at Red Deer Crossing in 1882. He returned to Headingly, Manitoba the following year and made the journey back the same summer, accompanied this time by his brothers, eight other families, a threshing machine, a sawmill, a steam boiler and an engine. The group settled east of Waskasoo Creek near the forests of huge spruce and poplar. By September, the sawmill was ready to meet the needs of a growing settlement along the Red Deer River.

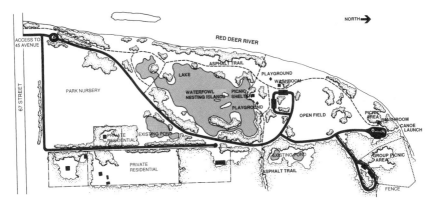

The milled lumber sold for between $20 and $30 for a thousand feet in 1884. The demand for houses and buildings often outstripped the supply even though the mill operated almost continuously, at times even around the clock. A competitor, the Alberta Lumber Company, tried, through political influence, to have the McKenzie sawmill closed down. The news caused an uproar in the community: 77 settlers signed a petition and sent it to the Department of the Interior, then responsible for timber leases. The mill resumed operation shortly afterwards and continued to operate into the mid-1890s.

The sawmill wasn't the end of their enterprise: by 1886 the McKenzies had built and were running a ferry across the Red Deer a little farther downstream. When a traffic bridge was proposed for the Red Deer townsite, the McKenzies won the construction contract. They also travelled from farm to farm during harvest time with their threshing machine.

In 1889, Benjamin died. The following year Roderick relocated to Beaverhill Lake before heading north to the Klondike to search for gold with brother David. Both eventually returned to Alberta, no richer than when they had left.

The McKenzie Trail area was more recently used as a garbage dump, by a gravel company and the Red Deer Trap and Skeet Club. The city's tree farm occupies the former shooting range. Where geese and ducks paddle serenely on an island-studded pond, gravel was mined until the 1950s. The rehabilitation of these gravel pits was made possible through the provincial Reclamation Program funded by Alberta's Heritage Savings Trust Fund. Beyond the pond and stretching toward the river, now the site of a picnic area, was the nuisance ground for the city. Just below the escarpment are a handful of acreages. Further development of housing is not permitted since the area is prone to flooding in times of very high water.

Balsam poplar.

This park area has an interesting natural side to it as well. The east side of the park is bordered by a steep, but forested, escarpment. The west side ends at the river. In between is a landscape of ridges and shallow depressions called swales covering a point bar. A point bar forms when a river rounds a curve. Its speed of flow drops as it hits the curve, much like a driver entering a twisty section of road. As it slows, its ability to carry sediments—silt, sand and gravel—also decreases. These sediments drop out at the inside of the curve where the river's flow is the slowest. Gradually, the sediments build up until they break the surface of the water as a projection of the former riverbank. During years of high water, the river's waves wash over this projection and deposit yet more sediments. Slowly the projection, or point bar, grows, stretching ever farther into the river. The river, in turn, is pushed away from that riverbank and toward the outside of the curve where it erodes the bank.

So where do the ridges and swales come into the picture? There are several theories for these land features, but all revolve around changes in the amount of water flow. Once the ridges start to form, subsequent floods enlarge them. Willows begin to grow on the ridges and during high water, trap more sediments, making the ridges grow. The flood waters scour the swales, thus deepening them. The best places to see these miniature peaks and valleys are between the riverbank and the trail and where the paved trail enters the forest near the first picnic area. The swale on either side of the trail is marshy in this spot and easy to recognize.

The paved trail extends from the grassy meadows of the park, through shrub communities full of willows and red-osier dogwood to a balsam poplar woodland. Some of the oldest trees in the park, balsam poplar and white spruce over a century old, grow here. Where the balsam have died and fallen, white spruce, the climax species in this type of forest, have taken over. The transition is as easy to feel as it is to see. On a hot, sunny day, the meadows seem to shimmer with heat. As you continue into the verge of the forest, the air becomes cooler and progressively more moist. The buzz of bees is left behind, but now the warbles and trills of numerous small, secretive birds can be heard. Leaving the shrub belt, you enter under the pillars of the tall balsam. There is still some sunlight that reaches the ground and splashes of colour from many different wildflowers break up the green. The air is cooler yet. When you reach the base of the escarpment, the balsam give way to white spruce and the sun peeks in only where there is a slight opening in the tree canopy. Few plants live in the cool, shady environment beneath these rough-barked conifers: some young spruce, a few leggy shrubs and a scatter of twinflower, bishop's cap and one-sided wintergreen.

McKenzie Trail is the best place in the city to see the succession from meadow to spruce forest, although it is taking place throughout the park. If there were to be no floods, no fires, no changes in climate and no logging or selective cutting, all the park areas would eventually, after hundreds of years, be covered by white spruce.

McKenzie Trail.

Areas like this, where there is a variety of plant life and habitat, are very attractive to wildlife. Some parts of the area provide food, others shelter from the weather and others hiding places from natural predators and people. Mule deer and white-tailed deer move up and down the escarpment from the farm fields above through the variety of forests to the open lands near the river. Coyote and fox hunt ground squirrels and mice in the meadows and swift snowshoe hare among the willows and poplars.

The main pond near the group picnic area is a perfect spot for the beginner birder. Each year, dozens of Canada geese congregate there, some raising their families on the islands and staying all summer. These geese are the ultimate nannies: while one adult remains at the ponds with sometimes 20 or 30 goslings, the rest eat out. Red-necked grebes, a very shy and easily disturbed bird, can be seen up close from the wooden deck or the road. Their haunting cackle of a call will send shivers down your spine!

A beaver has built a lodge near the bridge and its winter food stash of tender, young branches is anchored in the mud nearby. Muskrat patrol the pond, their long, thin tails drawing Ss in their wake. Their favourite food is the roots of the cattails growing along the water's edge. Red-winged blackbirds hang their nests from the cattail stems and while the brown females tend to their young, the males flex their crimson epaulettes and sing lustily from nearby trees.

An afternoon or a day spent cycling the paved path to the top of the escarpment or through the woods and meadows followed by a rest in one of the picnic areas by the pond or the river makes for a fine outing.

Highland Green and the Pines Escarpment

Access
Highland Green trails can be accessed from Kerry Wood Drive above Bower Ponds, at Howarth Close or behind North Elementary School, and south of the Safeway in Parkland Mall
Pines Escarpment Trail can be accessed at 67th Street, from Parsons Close, Piper Drive, Page Avenue and 77th Street, and from the North Bank Trail
Facilities: none
Environment: aspen forest to the west, white spruce forest in the east
Common Plants
Highland Green: aspen poplar, Manitoba maple, sweet clover, snowberry, saskatoon, chokecherry, asters, goldenrod, northern bedstraw
Pines Escarpment: white spruce, bishop's cap, one-sided wintergreen, horsetail, bunchberry
Common Animals: woodpeckers, chickadees, house sparrow, nuthatches, waxwings, black-billed magpie, least chipmunk, deer mouse, red fox, coyote, snowshoe hare
Special Features: old spruce forest

Highland Green

The Highland Green Trail is actually two unconnected trails following the northern escarpment of the valley. The most westerly section, starting above Bower Ponds, intersects the old railway right-of-way before heading northeast through a narrow belt of mature aspen woods backing the Oriole Park subdivision. Before reaching Taylor Drive, the trail opens onto a grassy slope, well used in winter for tobogganing.

The middle section of the Highland Green Trail extends from Howarth Close and drops to the valley floor near North Elementary School. This stretch offers a more pleasant way of climbing out of the Fairview district than following the road.

Pines Escarpment

Part of the Pines Escarpment Trail begins on the grassy slope below the south end of Parkland Mall. This portion of the trail skirts the edge of the mall parking lot on the south and east and passes the top of Red Deer's first ski hill. Saskatoon and chokecherry afficionados would find this trail very interesting in July. This area was the scene of military artillery training exercises from the 1920s to the 1950s.

The trail reaches 67th Street, which should be crossed at the traffic lights to the west to continue along the trail.

A gravel trail follows the edge of the escarpment from 67th Street to 77th Street. Parts of the trail follow the old railway grade and timbers, bridges and other railroad debris can be seen. The railway moved to the valley floor from the unstable valley wall to prevent slippage of the tracks. The trail passes through a forest of white spruce, not pine as suggested by the name. In fact, there are no naturally occurring pine trees in Waskasoo Park. The Pines area was once known as Les Sapins, the Spruces, by the predominantly French community of North Red Deer. The name became corrupted over time, leaving the misnomer, the Pines.

The dense canopy of the tall spruce permits little sunlight to reach the forest floor. For most of the extent of this trail, there is very little undergrowth. Bishop's cap, twinflower, bunchberry, one-sided wintergreen, feather mosses and dog's tooth lichen cover the forest floor with hues of green. Anywhere that a tree has fallen or a sewer or gas line right-of-way has cut a swath through the forest and let the light in, an explosion of growth occurs. Here you may find bearberry, grasses, wild rose, snowberry, honeysuckle, columbine, and other shrubs and wildflowers.

The abundance of plant life mirrors the numbers and variety of wildlife. In winter, the tracks of snowshoe hare often cross the path. The jumping track patterns of red squirrel and least weasel tell interesting stories of the hunted and the hunter. Deer mice and red-backed voles hide under the snow in hushed tunnels, raising families and hoping to remain undetected by the keen-nosed weasel or a hungry great horned owl.

Birds, too, frequent the spruce woods. Chickadees are most common, flitting about in search of insects hidden under bark or tucked into a hanging leaf. Red and white-winged crossbills, with their perfectly adapted beaks, open cones and extract the seeds. Blue jays squawk overhead

Black-capped chickadee.

and, in summer, kinglets flutter in the treetops. Both winter and summer, the sombre spruce forest is full of life.

Several openings in the forest allow a view of the river valley. To the east, backing the Gaetz Lakes Sanctuary and McKenzie Trail Recreation Area, is another escarpment. The two escarpments mark the plain where a young Red Deer River once flowed. The river has cut through sediments deposited by a glacial lake, by ice sheets and by ancient rivers, carving the valley we know today. It continues to excavate its bed and change the valley. Can you imagine what this valley will look like 100 years from now? 10,000 years from now?

Three Mile Bend Recreation Area

Access: from Riverside Drive, 77 Street east, by bicycle or on foot from North Bank Trail, or from River Bend Golf Course and Recreation Area

Facilities: picnic areas, washrooms, canoe launch, canoe ponds, archery range, radio controlled car racetrack, freestyle skiing training jump, retriever dog training site, only park area where dogs are allowed off leash, five kilometres of paved trails

Environment: disturbed/partially reclaimed, small spruce forest, riverine

Common Plants: white spruce, juniper, snowberry, chokecherry, saskatoon, wild rose, harebell, aster, willow, horsetail, red–osier dogwood, coltsfoot

Common Animals: coyote, mule deer, porcupine, Canada goose, common merganser, osprey, bufflehead, goldeneye, merlin

Special Features: dogs–off–leash, recreational opportunities, osprey nest, waterfowl, rehabilitated gravel pits

Three Mile Bend is the place to go for recreation and wildlife viewing. A paved trail for walkers and cyclists forms a loop around this river meander. Those interested in other sports can bring a canoe, try some archery or work their dog. No equipment rentals or drinking water are available at the site, so bring your own. Although the freestyle skiing jump is only available to skiers who have mastered the rudiments of this

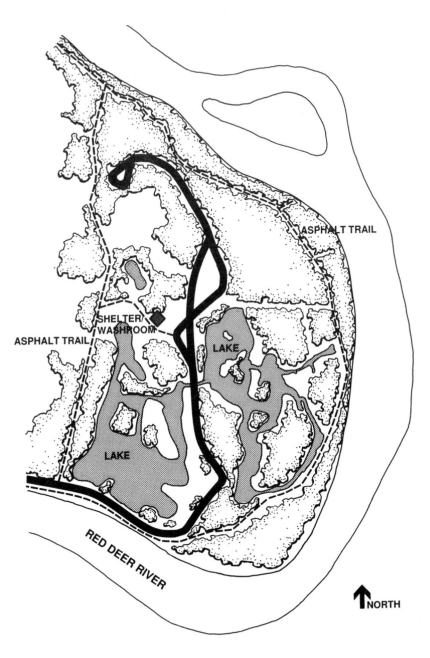

ASPHALT TRAIL

SHELTER
WASHROOM

ASPHALT TRAIL

LAKE

LAKE

RED DEER RIVER

NORTH

RED DEER'S SNOW ACROBATS

When you watch freestyle skiers on the slopes, their manoeuvres look polished and so easy to do. But the training for this fast growing sport is rigorous. Alberta's provincial freestyle team members, as well as skiers from across Canada, converge on the three jumps and the trampoline at Three Mile Bend each summer. Training begins on weekends in mid–May and continues until the end of September.

The athletes climb to the top of the towers, dip their skis in a biodegradable soap solution, then slide down the wet ramp. They execute their jumps over the water, then land safely in the pond, ready to try again. These aerialists must perform their jumps flawlessly over water, under the guidance of a certified coach, before they are allowed to attempt any jump on snow. In winter, the skiers train at the Canyon Ski Area and at Fortress Mountain.

Red Deer has produced a number of excellent skiers who have advanced to the provincial and national freestyle ski teams. Many more are in training and should be making a showing in the medals in the years to come.

Olympic demonstration sport, and who are admitted by the local freestyle ski club, spectators are welcome. Many events are sponsored by the local club; it can be contacted at 403-343–3997 or through its members.

Three Mile Bend was mined for its gravel until the late 1970s. The pits created by this resource extraction now serve as the interconnected canoe ponds. This park area shows just how successfully an industrial area can be rehabilitated to serve another, and very different, community need.

While dogs and their masters stroll below, an osprey keeps watch from its nest perched on top of a power pole. Osprey are large fish–eating birds that usually shy away from humans and especially urban areas, yet the osprey have been coming to Three Mile Bend for over 20 years. Originally they nested on top of an active power pole. After the power went out one time too many, Red Deer Electric, Light and Power installed a separate pole with a nesting platform for the osprey. The osprey weren't easily deterred and E, L & P tried installing another pole. Two nests can now be seen. Usually osprey raise a family in at least one of the nests; but don't be surprised if the dark bird leaps off its nest, long neck extended, and honks loudly as it heads for the

river. Canada geese have also taken a liking to the nesting platforms and some years, it's the early goose that gets the pole! Once ready to leave the nest for the river, the young also take the jump and usually land on the ground without being hurt.

The osprey fish in the river nearby, catching a wriggling dinner with their claws. After placing the fish facing head forward between its talons, the bird flies back to its nest or a nearby perch to enjoy its catch.

The curve in the river with its shallow rapids often has open water long after winter has covered other stretches with an icy veneer. Canada goose, common merganser and many different types of duck linger in these food–rich waters on their way south.

Three Mile Bend is one of the wilder areas of the park. The mixture of aspen forest, shrubland, grassland and spruce forest provide a variety of habitats and cover for deer, coyote, fox, snowshoe hare and other animals. Both sides of the river here are part of a natural highway used by wildlife to move up and down the valley. Wildlife corridors like these are important in sustaining a healthy population of animals. These corridors allow them to move to new food sources, to find unrelated mates and to escape from predators. Most importantly, wildlife can move safely through the city in the river or creek valleys without having to cross any roads. Through the foresight of city managers and the citizens of Red Deer, nowhere in the city is there development right to the water's edge. Red Deer is a safe place for wildlife.

River Bend Golf Course and Recreation Area

Access: from 30th Avenue, by bicycle or on foot from Riverside Drive and Three Mile Bend Recreation Area

Facilities: 18–hole championship golf course, mini–links, putting greens, driving range, picnic area, canoe launch, biathlon range, hiking and cross–country skiing trails, pro shop, club house, rentals, lessons

Environment: man–made, spruce forest, riverine

Common Plants: white spruce, snowberry, bunchberry, juniper, bearberry, twinflower, horsetail

Common Animals: mule deer, white–tailed deer, coyote, red fox, red squirrel, least weasel, beaver, woodpeckers, waterfowl, great horned owl, saw–whet owl

Special Features: Discovery Canyon water playground, par 72 golf course, old balsam and white spruce forests

River Bend appeals to all members of the family: there is golfing for youth and adults, a water playground with gentle rapids and pools for the youngsters, and a picnic site and walking trails for all. Many pleasant hours can be spent here both in summer and in winter when the trails appeal to novice and expert cross–country skiers alike.

Golfers come from across Western Canada to play and compete at this par 72 championship course. Each of the 18 holes has three tees, designed

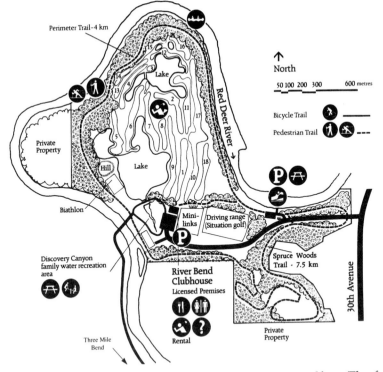

to accommodate beginner, intermediate and expert golfers. The front tees total 4950 metres (5,550 yards) in length, while the back tees stretch for 5806 metres (6,451 yards). The course offers a challenge to all players regardless of their skill level, with 11 waterholes, 58 sand traps and two lakes just waiting to swallow a golf ball or two.

Novices can practise their swings on the nine–hole mini–links before graduating to the main course. All golfers can hone their skills on the practice putting greens or the driving range. And, no matter what level you are at, golf lessons with a pro are available through the city's Recreation and Culture Department or at the club house.

After a round, golfers can relax at the club house, enjoy a meal in the restaurant and browse in the pro shop. Power carts, pull carts and golf clubs can be rented here, too.

While the adults golf, kids can splash and swim at Discovery Canyon. Armed with an inflated tire tube or rubber mattress, they can ride the rapids and small waterfalls to a fountain pool at the bottom. The water never gets too deep or the rapids too dangerous for children to get hurt, if they behave appropriately. A sand beach along one edge of the pool is perfect for toddlers wanting to build castles. A grassy picnic area keeps the sand out of your sandwiches!

Canoeists can put in or take out at a launch near the east end of the recreation area. A float to the Highway 11 (Joffre) Bridge takes about four to six hours, depending on how vigorously you paddle. In spring, fast–flowing waters shave an hour or two off your total time. To canoe to River Bend from Great Chief Park, allow two to three hours; from Fort Normandeau, add another hour.

River Bend Recreation Area, as the name implies, sits on a flat river floodplain at a bend in the Red Deer River. The Perimeter Trail, four kilometres in length, follows the edge of the floodplain, and is a cool excursion no matter how hot the day. Huge balsam poplar trees thrive here in the moist soils of the riverbank. Willows reach out over the water, hiding the nests of warblers and marsh wrens and shading the statue–still great blue heron patiently contemplating a slippery meal. Magpies are common here; their raucous calls seem at odds with their beautiful, iridescent plumage.

The jewels of this forest are the wildflowers nestled below the red–stemmed dogwood bushes. Western Canada violet, fairy bells, star–flowered Solomon's seal, one–sided wintergreen, wild lily–of–the–valley and early blue violet have simple but striking little flowers that are worth looking for. Later in the summer, goldenrod, fireweed and asters add new colours to the forest palette.

While white spruce are common along the Perimeter Trail, embarking on the 7.5 kilometre Spruce Woods Trail thrusts you deep among these evergreen giants. The trail winds past beaver dams, up and down hills and leads to eye–catching vistas of the Red Deer River valley. Deer mice and least weasel inhabit brush piles left over from trail construction. Accompanied by

the chatter of a red squirrel or the cheerful song of a chickadee, the hiker may chance upon a ruffed grouse, a mule deer or a snowshoe hare.

The two trails are usually trackset in the winter for cross–country skiers. A nominal trail fee is charged to users. The Perimeter Trail is the easier of the two. The hills on the Spruce Woods Trail are challenging. Make sure you can snowplow and ski downhill under control before you attempt this one!

The Parkland Cross–Country Ski Club organizes provincial and local loppets at the golf course each winter. These are advertised through their club newsletter and in the local media.

The local biathlon club uses the golf course and biathlon range for practice and competitions. Club members can be reached through the Recreation and Culture Department.

Gravel Mining

Gravel helped to pay for this recreation area. While the park was being developed, the rich gravel beds here were excavated and the gravel sold. The funds were used to develop the golf course, hiking trails, Discovery Canyon and other amenities. The gravel pits can still be seen holding the water destined for the water playground, irrigation and other uses.

The gravel found here originated in the Rocky Mountains to the west. As the mountains were forming, great rivers eroded the rising peaks and tumbled the rock downhill onto the plains of Central Alberta. The ancient waterways spread thick layers of gravel across the flatlands, filling in any ripples in the landscape. (*See The Land Through Time.*)

More to Explore

Within an easy drive of Red Deer are places to explore for an hour, a day or even longer. Retrace the paddle strokes of the voyageurs and experience the fur trade, become a farmer for a day and get close to a cow or a steam–driven tractor, or enjoy the fresh air and a little bit of exercise as you follow a path through meadows and forests. You will find a list of interesting sites and attractions below. Most are within an hour's drive of Red Deer; driving times are approximate. The sites are divided into four sections, depending upon their location from Red Deer. For example, Aspen Beach Provincial Park is located in the northwest of Red Deer section. The sections are roughly bounded by Highway 11 east and west and Highway 2 north and south. You may wish to check with the sites showing seasonal hours about their current times and dates of opening before you head out, or stop at or call (403-346–0180) the Visitor Information Centre at Heritage Ranch where guides to Central Alberta attractions are available.

Enjoy your discoveries!

Red Deer Canyon.

Northeast of Red Deer

Red Deer Canyon

Access: Highway 11 east for nine kilometres, then follow the signs for three kilometres; by canoe from River Bend Golf Course or Burbank

The Red Deer Canyon is one of the most breathtaking natural sites near Red Deer. During the last glacial advance between two million and 10,000 years ago, the Red Deer River was diverted from its north–northeast trending valley. It began to flow eastward, where it gouged through a ridge of land known locally as Divide Hill. At its deepest point, the resulting canyon measures 210 metres (700 feet) in depth. The canyon was visited by some of the first Europeans exploring the west; a fur trader's signature was found carved into sandstone cliffs nearby.

The canyon is worth a visit any time of year, but particularly in the fall when the dazzling display of yellow aspens, green white spruce and red saskatoons and chokecherries will mesmerize any photographer, amateur or professional. The canyon was once considered for a national park. Timber leases amounting to an estimated four million board feet won over preservation.

Red Deer Canyon is the site of the Canyon Ski Area with 11 runs, two chairs (triple and double), two T–bars, a rope tow, a lodge, ski school, ski equipment shop and 150 metres (500 feet) of vertical. In summer, trail rides depart near the river and children can participate in week-long camps. For skiing information call 403-346–5588 and for trail rides call 403-346–5589.

Rt. Hon. Roland and Norah Michener.

Michener House, Lacombe

Access: Highways 2 or 2A north; 5036 – 51 Street in Lacombe
Contact: Maski–pitoon Historical Society —403-782-3933
Open: Year-round

Michener House is the birthplace of former Governor–General Daniel Roland Michener (1900–1991). The 'jogging Governor–General', as he was affectionately called, was well loved by Canadians everywhere. Involved in politics from his early 30s, Michener held provincial office in Ontario before moving into the federal arena where he served as Speaker of the House for five years. When the Conservative government was defeated, Michener went on to serve on a royal commission, then as High Commissioner to India and Ambassador to Nepal. In 1967, Michener became Governor-General, a position he held for seven years.

Michener House was built in 1894 to serve as a manse for the Methodist minister. The Micheners moved to the bustling village of Lacombe in 1899. The building had several owners after the Micheners moved to Red Deer and each one changed it to suit their needs. In 1977, the house was declared a Provincial Historic Resource and its painstaking restoration to its turn-of-the-century appearance was begun. Displays in the house depict Michener's personal life and political career as well as Lacombe's archives.

While in Lacombe, take note of the town's distinctive Edwardian architecture and the flatiron building, one of only three such structures in Alberta. Nearby is the Agricultural Research Station with hedging displays, tours and a picnic area.

Burbank

Access: From Highway 2A, turn east on Secondary Highway 597
Contact: Lacombe Fish and Game Association—403-885-5335
Open: Seasonally

Burbank Park is operated by the Lacombe Fish and Game Association. This pretty, seasonal campsite and picnic area is located at the confluence of the Blindman and Red Deer rivers and has been visited by picnickers since the

1920s. The Blindman River, from Highway 2A to the campground, is a favourite spring trip for experienced, local canoeists. Fishermen often try their luck for goldeye, walleye, pike and mountain whitefish. The cliffs and banks of the river have yielded some interesting palaeontological finds, including fossil plants and fish. (*See The Land Through Time.*) If you should spot any fossils, please leave them where you find them.

A hydroelectric dam was built on this site in 1904 by the Wilkins brothers (*see Bower Ponds and Great Chief Park.*) Dependent upon large volumes of water to operate, the hydroelectric operation did not succeed: the river all but disappears during the summer. The ruins of the powerhouse are still visible near the mouth of the river. While not a great source for power generation, the Blindman River did supply many local people with stones for house foundations.

J. J. Collett Natural Area
Access: From Highway 2 north of Lacombe, turn east on Milton Road. After 4.8 kilometres (three miles), turn north and proceed 6.4 kilometres (four miles); turn west to reach the entrance
Contact: 403-782–6138
Open: Year-round
The Collett Natural Area offers 18 kilometres of hiking trails through rolling terrain. Located within the aspen parkland, this area of sandy soils encompasses grasslands, aspen and balsam poplar forests, willow shrubland, black spruce peatland, willow–sedge wetland and white spruce communities. This quarter section of land harbours a wealth of wildlife, including white–tailed deer, coyote, porcupine, snowshoe hare, woodchuck, pocket gopher, great horned owl, ruffed grouse, yellow–bellied sapsucker, northern flicker, and several species of warbler and sparrow. Boreal chorus frog and wood frogs are especially vocal in the spring.

This site is used by local schools and Scouts for environmental education and orienteering.

Ellis Bird Farm
Access: From Highway 2A, turn east on Secondary Highway 597 near Blackfalds, then turn north on the Prentiss Road. Ellis Bird Farm is located west of the Union Carbide Prentiss Plant
Contact: 403-346–2211
Open: Mid–June to mid–August in the afternoon. Other visits by pre-arrangement only.
The Ellis Bird Farm was started by Charlie and Winnie Ellis. Long–time residents of the area, this brother and sister took great pains to look after the bird life around them. As bluebirds disappeared from surrounding

farmlands, due largely to competition from other native and non–native birds, the Ellises undertook a private crusade to save these beautiful birds. As you drive to the site, you will notice bird boxes becoming more and more numerous. The Ellises built hundreds of boxes for the cavity nesting bluebirds and placed them in appropriate habitat on their own and neighbouring fencelines. Their commitment to the bluebird has resulted in a comeback of this species and inspired others to create bluebird box trails throughout Alberta. This area of the County of Lacombe has the largest concentration of mountain bluebirds in the province.

The Ellises sold their land to Union Carbide on the condition that bluebird conservation continue at the site. The Red Deer River Naturalists negotiated with the company on behalf of the Ellises to preserve part of the land as a sanctuary and study area. The company provides a generous annual grant to a management board composed of naturalists, county representatives and Union Carbide officials. The board, in turn, has undertaken numerous public education projects and hired a biologist to undertake on–going studies of cavity nesters.

Mirror Museum
Access: From Highway 12 east of Lacombe, turn northeast on Highway 50
Contact: 403-788–3828
Open: Seasonally
The Mirror and District Museum houses displays about the railway and pioneer history of the area. Of particular interest are the CN railroad station office, a pioneer kitchen, blacksmith and automotive tools, and a series of photo albums depicting Mirror's heritage. The original St. Monica's Anglican Church, built in 1895 of logs and clad with siding, is located on the museum property. St. Monica's is one of the oldest standing churches in the province. The museum and Mirror residents host the annual Heritage Day festivities on the first weekend of August.

Northwest of Red Deer

Aspen Beach Provincial Park
Access: Highway 2 north to Highway 12, turn west and head 14 kilometres toward Bentley
Contact: 403-748–3939
Open: Park—year-round, campground only seasonally.
Aspen Beach was established in 1932 as one of Alberta's first provincial parks. Located on the southern tip of Gull Lake, the park is known primarily for its beach, campgrounds and swimming. Pike, whitefish and pickerel attract fishermen both summer and winter.

The southwest edge of the lake is marshy, providing habitat for spawning fish, frogs and numerous water birds. Birdwatchers will find plenty of species hiding among the marsh vegetation, in the willow thickets and in the mature poplar forest. Small mammals—chipmunk, skunk, flying squirrel—inhabit the forest, while muskrats patrol the marsh and lakeshore.

Of interest are the active sand dunes in the main park area. These dunes are slowly creeping southward, burying trees and shrubs in their way.

A one kilometre loop trail introduces walkers to the plants and animals of the area. A viewing platform perches over the marsh and is an ideal spot to observe birds and insects. Visit the Beach Centre for more information or join a ranger for the public programs available in the summer. Two campgrounds linked by a trail accommodate overnight visitors to the park.

Sylvan Lake Provincial Park

Access: Highway 11 or 11A west from Red Deer
Contact: 403-887-5522
Open: Year-round
The town of Sylvan Lake is a resort community on the south shore of Sylvan Lake. Cottages and summer camps surround the lake on all sides, except where provincial parks, a natural area and farmlands hug the shore.

Sylvan Lake Provincial Park is a long strip of land between the lake and Highway 11A through town. This day–use park provides access to 1.5 kilometres of sandy beach. Most of the park consists of lawns with poplar trees providing shade. Washrooms are located throughout the park, while concessions and a large playground can be found across the road. This park is particularly busy on summer weekends. The shallow, warm waters, largely free of weeds, leeches and the organism that causes swimmer's itch, are ideal for families with small children. Windsurfers and boaters often use the east end of the park. Boat rentals are available nearby for cruising, fishing and waterskiing, and there's a waterslide nearby. Lake cruises are offered. Fishermen may catch pike, whitefish, burbot and pickerel. Sylvan Lake's lighthouse can be seen from most of the lakeshore.

Jarvis Bay Provincial Park

Access: Highway 11A west of Red Deer to the edge of Sylvan Lake, then five kilometres north on Highway 20
Contact: 403-887-5522
Open: Park—year-round, campground only seasonally.
Campers wishing to overnight at Sylvan Lake often stay at neighbouring Jarvis Bay Provincial Park. This park overlooks the lake from high cliffs on Sylvan's eastern shore. The park is situated in a dense forest of aspen poplars where mule and white–tailed deer, fox, chipmunk and skunk may be spotted. Woodchucks make their homes near the cliffs, as do the garter snakes for which this area was once known. The park is a birdwatcher's paradise, with both woodland and wetland birds abundant. Water birds are best seen before the long weekend in May and after the Labour Day weekend when there is little boat traffic.

Sylvan Lake Natural Area

Access: Highway 11A west to the edge of Sylvan Lake, Highway 20 north for 6.9 kilometres, west for 11.2 kilometres, then south for one kilometre to the parking lot
Contact: For more information, contact Alberta Public Lands Division

in Ponoka at 403-783–7090 or the natural area's stewards, the Red Deer River Naturalists at 403-347–8200

Open: Year-round

This small natural area, one of over 100 such areas of protected public land in Alberta, is the only public land on the lakeshore still in its natural state. Within its 11 hectares are mature poplar forest, cattail and bulrush beds, and a zone of willows. A natural levee traps water and forms a sheltered lagoon where marsh plants grow. The moist woodland areas harbour several boreal forest plant species, including lady fern and oak fern, at the southern limit of their ranges.

White–tailed deer, moose and snowshoe hare frequent the forest, while muskrats and boreal chorus and wood frogs inhabit the shoreline. The natural area is home to abundant bird life, from pileated woodpeckers in the woods to western grebes offshore.

David Thompson Highway—Highway 11

The David Thompson Highway stretches from Red Deer to the Rocky Mountains and Banff National Park. This paved, all-weather road is worth a trip in itself. Named after the fur trader and explorer David Thompson, the highway leads to Rocky Mountain House where Thompson established a trading post and beyond, into the wild country he explored and mapped. It passes through croplands to Sylvan Lake, past pastures full of dairy and beef cattle, to the edge of the foothills near Crimson Lake.

Continuing westward, the highway rolls through forests of tamarack, black spruce, white spruce and lodgepole pine. Names like Horburg, Saunders and Alexo bring to mind the hectic days of railway construction when the Brazeau coal fields at Nordegg were being opened up. Unlike Nordegg, little is left of these old towns. Nordegg is the site of a coal mining town and tours of the townsite and mine buildings are available. The road travels past numerous campgrounds and recreation areas, skirts Abraham Lake, the reservoir behind the Bighorn Dam, and follows the North Saskatchewan River to the Banff National Park boundary.

Many opportunities for hiking, sightseeing, camping, fishing, trail riding, rafting, canoeing and exploring our past are available along this route. The David Thompson Highway is a prime wildlife watching area, with large mammals such as moose, elk, deer and bighorn sheep often feeding near roadsides. The many lakes and bogs are home to beaver, muskrat, mink and waterfowl. For more information on this area, read on or contact information centres in Red Deer (403-346–0180) or Rocky Mountain House (403-845–2414 in summer only) for a tourist guide, circle driving tour information and other literature. See *David Thompson Highway: A Hiking Guide* by Jane Ross and Dan Kyba.

Rocky Mountain House Museum
Access: Rocky Mountain House at 4604 – 49 Avenue, one block west of Highway 11
Contact: 403-845–2788
Open: Year-round
Step back to the turn of the century among artifacts and displays recreating the life of early settlers. Interesting exhibits include a 1920s classroom, a fully restored forestry cabin, as well as a range of personal and household items. A gift shop stocks arts and crafts and books on Alberta's history.

Crimson Lake Provincial Park
Access: Highway 11 west past Rocky Mountain House
Contact: 403-845–2340
Open: Park—year-round, campground seasonally and for winter camping.
Named by a local trapper for spectacular sunsets reflected in the lake's waters, Crimson Lake is a popular park among campers, swimmers, boaters, fishermen and cross–country skiers. The park is set in a transition zone between the foothills and the boreal forest to the north. It hosts plant and animal species from both regions, with over 100 different birds, 31 mammals and 266 vascular plants to keep naturalists busy! The park is a mixture of water bodies and woodlands. Crimson Lake is the largest of the

lakes, with a maximum depth of 10 metres. Bogs and marshes are inhabited by beaver, mink and muskrats, and visited by moose. Mule deer and white–tailed deer, as well as black bear and wolf, live in forests of lodgepole pine, white spruce, black spruce, aspen and balsam poplar.

In summer, enjoy swimming and sunbathing, hiking the 13 kilometres of trail, exploring the park with an Adventure Pack or looking at displays in the Visitor Centre. Guided walks, programs at the Hearth and the Amphitheatre, and special events are offered in the summer. In winter, bring your cross–country skis for the groomed, packed trails, or snowshoes can be borrowed at the park office for off–trail exploration. Try ice fishing for rainbow trout at Twin Lakes.

Rocky Mountain House National Historic Park
Access: Highway 11A, five kilometres west from Rocky Mountain House
Contact: 403-845–2412
Open: Seasonally
Alberta's only national historic park, Rocky Mountain House was the site of five different fur trade posts between 1799 and 1875. David Thompson and other explorers pushed west from this site in search of fur reserves and new routes to the west.

Visitors will find a visitor centre with interpretive exhibits covering the fur trade, exploration of the west and native peoples. Outside, a trail takes you past the remains of the forts, a Red River cart, a York boat, a cemetery, bison paddock and teepees. At the demonstration site you may be able to take part in an activity from the past.

Nordegg Heritage Centre
Access: Highway 11, 92 kilometres west of Rocky Mountain House
Contact: 403-845–4444
Open: Seasonally
The Brazeau Coal Fields were discovered in 1907 by Martin Nordegg, of a German development company. Rich seams of coal provided a livelihood for over 2,500 residents of the isolated, but very modern, town of Nordegg. Of interest is the town's layout, which followed the semi-circular pattern of Mount Royal in Quebec. The reign of coal lasted but 50 years—when gas was discovered in abundance elsewhere, the demand for coal to fuel railway locomotives plummeted.

Today only some of the mine buildings and equipment remain. The Nordegg Heritage Centre and its exhibits is the point of departure for a guided tour of the mine site, including the miners' wash house, mine entrance and the briquetting plant. The Nordegg Historic Heritage Interest Group is stabilizing and restoring the structures.

Ram River Falls

Access: 50 kilometres south from Highway 11
Contact: Alberta Forestry Service—403-845-8272
Ram River Falls is a spectacular end to a drive through rolling foothills and dark forests. The Ram River cascades over a bedrock lip to plunge to a pool far below. The slanting bedrock and sheer talus slopes join with the shimmering waters and the often–present rainbow to delight those who take the 10 minute-long walk to the viewpoint. Bighorn sheep rams, the river's namesake, are usually found near the entrance to the recreation area. Moose, deer and elk can often be seen in the campground.

Bighorn Dam

Access: Highway 11, 32 kilometres west past Nordegg at the north end of Abraham Lake
Contact: 403-721–3952
Open: Seasonally
The Bighorn Dam is one of the largest earth–filled dams in Western Canada. The electricity generated here by TransAlta Utilities is used all the way to Edmonton. A small interpretive centre near the dam houses displays on power generation.

Kootenay Plains Ecological Reserve

Access: Highway 11, 150 kilometres west of Rocky Mountain House
Contact: 403-843–2545
Open: Year-round
The Kootenay Plains is a 3204 hectares (8,010 acre) area at the head of Abraham Lake. This reserve protects land representative of the montane, a low valley ecosystem found in the Rocky Mountains. It contains many special features including several plant species found nowhere else or at the limit of their distribution. The plains are also an important wintering ground for elk and deer.

David Thompson notes in his journal that traders from Rocky Mountain House would meet here with the Kootenay Indians to trade.

Siffleur Falls

Access: Highway 11 west of Nordegg
Contact: Alberta Forest Service in Rocky Mountain House at 403-845–8250 or near Nordegg at 403-721–3965 for further information and maps.

Open: Weather permitting
There is an easy four kilometre-long hiking trail that crosses the North Saskatchewan River on a swinging footbridge, then continues parallel to the Siffleur River to a beautiful waterfall. The trail meanders through open country filled with wild flowers in June and July and fragrant with the scent of sun–warmed lodge-pole pines. This is one of the access routes into the Siffleur Wilderness Area.

Siffleur Falls.

Southwest of Red Deer

Markerville

Access: 40 kilometres from Red Deer, Highway 2 or 2A south to Highway 42 or 54, then follow signs

The hamlet of Markerville, on the Medicine River, is the only Icelandic settlement in Alberta. In 1888, Icelandic immigrants began to arrive from the Dakota Territory where they had first settled in North America. The Icelanders were attracted to Central Alberta by the area's isolation and natural riches. They established a settlement called 'Tindastoll', named after a mountain in their homeland. A second settlement called 'Hola' was established nearby. The Icelanders hoped to maintain their culture and language by living apart from other settlers and being self–sufficient. The families planted crops and gardens and raised cattle and sheep to meet their needs. The men often hired themselves out to sheep ranches and sawmills in an effort to make some cash for the family. Within a few years, the settlers had schools and a post office built and paid for by their labours.

In 1899, the Dominion government built a creamery. The area was renamed Markerville in honour of the dairy commissioner, C. P. Marker, who encouraged the establishment of the creamery. Markerville became the heart of the Icelandic community. The village thrived and soon a library, hotel and several stores served the populace. When the creamery closed in 1972, the economic mainstay of the community disappeared. Young people gradually left the area to look for opportunities elsewhere. Yet the history of Markerville is not forgotten. Fensala Hall exhibits many photographs from Markerville's early days. Several historic sites have been lovingly preserved, including the Markerville Creamery, the Markerville Lutheran Church and north of the hamlet, Stephansson House and Hola School. An historical walking and driving tour of the area is available from information centres or the Markerville Creamery. Don't miss the Centennial sculpture on the edge of town.

Old boy scouts may be interested in the privately owned Boy Scout Museum. Call ahead to make an appointment: 403-728–3262.

Markerville Creamery

Access: In Markerville
Contact: 403-728–3006
Open: Seasonally

In 1899, 34 local farmers formed the Tindastoll Butter and Cheese Manufacturing Association. The Dominion Government then established a creamery in Markerville, hiring a qualified buttermaker while the association took care of the building and equipment. In its first year, the creamery produced 24,664 pounds of butter from cream supplied by local farmers. Butter production grew dramatically and in 1902 a new building, the present-day Markerville Creamery, was built. Dan Morkeberg, and later his son Carl, was the buttermaker. Farmers brought in milk, then with the introduction of home separators, cream, to the creamery. The cream was weighed, sampled and graded to determine the amount of butterfat it contained and how much the farmer would be paid. Mondays were cheque days and everyone came into town to shop and chat with their neighbours.

The creamery operated until 1972. It lay abandoned until 1978, when it was declared a Provincial Historic Resource by the government of Alberta. In 1984, the Icelandic Society undertook the restoration of the creamery to its 1934 appearance. Today, visitors can see the equipment used to make butter, hear stories of the creamery days from old–timers, relax in the Kaffistofa for an authentic Icelandic meal, or snack or browse through the gift shop.

Stephansson House Provincial Historic Site
Access: Highway 2 or 2A south of Red Deer, then follow the signs
Contact: 403-728–3929 in summer, 403-361–1351 in winter
Open: Seasonally
Markerville's most notable resident was Stephan G. Stephansson. Born in 1853 in Iceland, Stephansson immigrated to the United States in 1873, eventually homesteading near Markerville in 1889. While a farmer by day, by night Stephansson wrote powerful verse about his new country, family, politics and nature. Long considered Iceland's national poet, Stephansson's work has now been translated into English and is gaining recognition in Canada.

Stephansson House is a Provincial Historic Site, open mid–May to Labour Day 10 am to 6 pm daily. The home of Stephansson until his death in 1927, the pink and green Victorian-style house has been restored and welcomes visitors. Costumed interpreters offer tours and programs and are eager to discuss Stephansson's life and works. A traditional Tombola is held every summer.

For more information, call 403-728–3006.

Innisfail Natural Area
Access: Highway 2 south from Red Deer, then Secondary Highway 590 east from Innisfail for 10 kilometres
Contact: Alberta Public Lands Division at 403-340–5451 or the Red Deer River Naturalists, the area's stewards, at 403-347–8200.
Open: Year-round

Once part of a homestead, the Innisfail Natural Area shows both uncultivated aspen parkland and areas of regrowth. Aspen and balsam poplar forest, wet willow shrubland and sedge meadows offer food and shelter to numerous animals including deer, moose, coyote, beaver, muskrat, grouse, hawks and an abundance of songbirds. The natural area is one of the few places in the aspen parkland belt that remains in a relatively natural state. A short trail leads from the road to the site, then animal trails can be followed through forests and meadows.

Dr. George/Kemp House
Access: In Innisfail at 5713 – 51 Avenue
Contact: 403-227–4881
Open: Hours vary
The beautifully restored Dr. George/Kemp House now serves as a tea room and showpiece. This century-old house was home to the area's first doctor, Dr. Henry George, and his wife, Barbara. Dr. George was a naturalist and a collector. He turned his home into a private museum to display a variety of artifacts and specimens, but like most collectors, he couldn't enjoy his finds alone; a year later his passion had become the Innisfail Museum. In 1907, Dr. George moved, lock, stock and museum to Red Deer, to continue his practice.

Barbara George was an artist. Her paintings hang in Calgary's Glenbow Museum and her most famous design is found in every provincial building in the province—the Alberta crest.

After the Georges left, the house was purchased by William and Katy Kemp. William died in 1920, leaving five sons in the care of his wife. Katy converted the house into a boardinghouse to support her young family. Eventually the house was sold, but saved from demolition by its designation as a Provincial Historic Resource. In 1992, the Dr. George/Kemp House Preservation Society took on the mammoth task of restoring the house to its 1920s appearance.

The house is handicapped accessible. You can stop in for tea at the Katy Jane Tea Room or just look around.

Innisfail and District Historical Village Museum
Access: Highway 2 or 2A south to Innisfail, then 2.5 blocks west of the water tower on 42 Street between 51 and 52 Avenues
Contact: 403-227–2906
Open: Seasonally
One of the largest outdoor museums in Central Alberta, the Village Museum includes 12 pioneer buildings housing exhibits on the area's past from the time of native use to the 1930s. A train station, houses, a store, a church and farm buildings each illustrate a different aspect of pioneer life. The showpiece is 'The Spruces', the only preserved stopping house from the days of stage coach travel between Calgary and Edmonton. The museum also has a tea room and a photo gallery. Visit from mid–May to Labour Day, Tuesday through Sunday from 8 am to 4:30 pm. Tea is served on Fridays between 2 pm and 4 pm.

Dickson Dam
Access: Highway 2 or 2A south from Red Deer, west on Highway 781, then follow the signs
Contact: 403-227–1106
Open: Seasonally
The construction of the Dickson Dam on the Red Deer River began in 1980. The reservoir created behind the dam, Gleniffer Lake, began storing water in 1983. This 40 metre-high and 650 metre-long earthfill structure releases water throughout the year to ensure a constant supply of water downstream.

Several day-use areas are located on the shores of Gleniffer Lake. Fishermen cast their lines for trout in the stocked pond. Swimming is not recommended. An interpretive centre explaining the workings of the dam is located at the dam edge.

Dickson Store Museum

Access: Highway 2 south of Red Deer, west on Highway 54, three kilometres south at Spruceview
Contact: 403-728–3355
Open: Seasonally

In 1903, five families and two single men arrived at a tract of homestead land where they were to establish a Danish colony. From this small group of 17 people grew a strong and close–knit community. Together with the others who came later, they cleared and drained the land, built homes and established the hamlet of Dickson. To preserve their past, the members of the Danish Heritage Society of Dickson restored the Dickson store as a pioneer museum. The store has been restored to its 1930s appearance, including an upstairs living quarters used by the Christiansen family.

Due to the historic nature of the hamlet and its old buildings and cemetery, Dickson has been chosen as the site of the proposed Danish Canadian National Museum and Archives. This museum will celebrate the contribution of Danes to Canada and include an exhibit area, library and archives. Using an historic Danish residential school on the site, the Danish Canadian National Museum Society will develop a small exhibit gallery, coffee shop and gift store. Outside, visitors will be able to explore several gardens, including a typical Danish garden, a pioneer garden and a children's garden based on Hans Christian Anderson's stories.

Medicine River Wildlife Rehabilitation Centre

Access: Highway 2 south to Highway 54; turn south at Raven and follow the signs
Contact: 403-346–9453
Open: Year-round

The Medicine River Wildlife Rehabilitation Centre is dedicated to rescuing and rehabilitating injured wildlife found between Calgary and Ponoka and the Rockies to the Saskatchewan border. Once their health is restored, the animals are retrained when necessary to survive in the wild and released where they were first found, whenever possible. Some animals injured beyond rehabilitation are retained by this licensed centre to act as foster parents to young animals or used by the staff in public programs.

The centre is located on gently rolling, treed land. Further development includes plans for more outdoor pens for the various species, trails and exhibits. Visitors can tour the main building and see some of the patients, but at this point, most of the exterior pens are out of bounds. The centre is open daily and can be contacted at 403-346–9453.

Raven Brood Trout Station
Access: Highway 2 south to Highway 54; turn south on Highway 22
Contact: 403-722–2180
Open: Year-round
Alberta Fish and Wildlife runs a brood station for rainbow and brook trout where fertilized eggs are collected then sent to hatcheries where the young trout are raised. These trout eventually are used to stock lakes for sport fishing in Alberta. The fish can be watched in exterior ponds and springs. A picnic area is also available.

Bowden Pioneer Museum
Access: Highway 2 south to Bowden, 2011 – 20 Avenue
Contact: 403-224–2122
Open: Seasonally
The Bowden Pioneer Museum displays a variety of artifacts from the pioneer days. Of note is the photographic collection of Gerald R. 'Bob' Hoare, who left a large bank of images chronicling life at the turn of the century.

Red Lodge Provincial Park
Access: Highway 2 south to Bowden, west on Highway 587
Contact: 403-224–3216
Open: Park—year-round, campground only seasonally.
Red Lodge Provincial Park is a quiet hideaway on the Little Red Deer River. This small water course meanders leisurely through the park,

cutting a swath through the old aspen and balsam poplar forest. Wildlife abounds here, with moose, deer and beaver being common sights. Over 70 bird species have also been recorded. While no official hiking trails exist, wildlife trails can be followed through the thin underbrush. Fishermen will find pike and suckers a common catch, although lake chub, trout and perch can be caught as well.

The park has a campground and playground. Picnicking is popular here and many visitors swim in the warm waters of the river.

Butcher Creek Natural Area

Access: Highway 2 south to Bowden, west on Highway 587 for 25 kilometres and north for three kilometres
Contact: Alberta Public Lands Division at 403-340–5451 or the Red Deer River Naturalists, the area's stewards, at 403-347–8200.
Open: Year-round

This natural area is typical of the aspen parkland. Located on the flood plain of the Red Deer River, the river flats are covered by a patchwork of old channels dammed by beavers and overhung by alders and willow, shallow depressions carpeted with sedges and other moisture–loving plants and cool spruce forests hugging shady banks. Drier uplands host aspen and balsam poplar forests and open meadows.

The variety of vegetation provides food and shelter for moose, deer, snowshoe hare, red squirrel, coyote, fox, mink, waterfowl and songbirds. Numerous hiking trails give access to all parts of this riverine environment.

Didsbury and District Museum and Cultural Centre

Access: Highway 2 south, turn west on Highway 582
Contact: 403-335–9295
Open: Year-round

The Didsbury Museum is located in the town's old school. It displays native, military and sports artifacts, and tells of the early pioneer days when Mennonites and later British immigrants settled in the area. Special travelling exhibits are often featured as well as local art.

Olds Mountain View Museum and Archives

Access: Highway 2 south to Highway 27, turn west; 5038 – 50 Street
Contact: 403-556–8464
Open: Seasonally

The Mountain View Museum preserves the memories of the pioneers who settled in this area. Many fascinating artifacts tell the story of the town's and the surrounding area's past.

The museum is one of the stops on the Olds Historical Walking Tour.

Olds College

Access: Highway 2 south, turn west on Highway 27; located at the junction of Highway 27 and 50 Street
Contact: 403-556–8281
Open: Year-round

There is lots to see at Olds College: historic structures such as the original horse barn, water tower and calf barn, original plantings, a hall of fame, livestock brand boards, a history of fashion mural and historic displays about the college. Tours can be arranged by calling 403-556–8281 in advance.

The college is the starting and ending point for the Olds Historical Walking Tour. The tour takes visitors past heritage homes, St. John's Anglican Church, the Mountain View Museum and other historical structures. The walking tour brochure is available at the Tourist Information Centre or at the Town Office at 4911 – 51 Avenue.

Sundre Museum and Pioneer Village

Access: Highway 2 south to Highway 27, turn west and continue for 40 kilometres
Contact: 403-638–3233
Open: Seasonally

The Sundre Museum owes much to its volunteers. Over the years it has restored a Norwegian log cabin, an old schoolhouse, blacksmith's shop and a barn. All buildings are furnished with appropriate and authentic artifacts to recreate the rich history of the Sundre area. Of interest are their exhibits on the lumber industry, particularly the Great West Lumber Company, which cut timber in the area, then floated the logs on the Red Deer River to their mill in Red Deer.

PaSu Farm
Access: Highway 2 south, turn west to Carstairs, then south on Highway 2A to Highway 580, continue west for eight kilometres, then south for 2.4 kilometres or follow the signs from Highway 2
Contact: 403-337–2800
Open: Year-round
PaSu Farm is a working sheep farm with the added attractions of a tea room and educational programs. There is a petting area for children and many different varieties of sheep are on display. The Canadian Classic Sheep Dog Trials are held at the farm.

Custom Woolen Mills
Access: Highway 2 south to Highway 581, then 24 kilometres following signs east and north
Contact: 403-337–2221
Open: Year-round
The Custom Woolen Mills is a working museum where raw wool is cleaned, carded, spun, dyed, and made into comforters and batts. The wool can be purchased at any point in the process. The mill uses carding machines dating from 1868 to 1910 and a spinning mule and knitting machine from 1910.

Southeast of Red Deer

Dry Island Buffalo Jump Provincial Park
Access: Highway 21 to Huxley, then east for 19 kilometres
Contact: 403-442–4211
Open: Seasonally
Dry Island Buffalo Jump is the most northerly area along the Red Deer River where badlands typical of the Drumheller area can be seen. The park is largely a wilderness area with no official trails through the grasslands and aspen bluffs. As you enter the park, stop at the pull off for

a breathtaking view of the valley. To the right is the cliff used by native peoples in buffalo hunts. Buffalo would be stampeded toward the edge of the cliff and, unable to stop and turn, would plummet over the edge. The base of the cliff and the valley floor have yielded rich archaeological finds, including projectile points, stone knives and the remains of successive encampments.

To the left from the viewpoint is the park's namesake, an island of rock separated from the valley wall by thousands of years of water and wind erosion. Across the river, the prairie is folded into coulees where spruce mingle with aspen poplars and mule deer and cougar hide.

Even though formal trails don't exist, the park is easy to explore on foot, or from the river by canoe. By June, the grasslands explode with crocus mauves, wild geranium pinks, gaillardia oranges, prickly pear cactus yellows and the white of saskatoon and snowberry.

A picnic under the shady balsam poplars and their varied birdlife is very pleasant. There is no campground, however, one can camp nearby at a private campground.

Slack Slough
Access: Next to Highway 2 at the south entrance to Red Deer
Contact: Alberta Fish and Wildlife Division—403-340–5142
Open: Year-round

Slack Slough is one of the best birdwatching areas near Red Deer. The 82.5 hectare area was developed by the Alberta government to enhance waterfowl production. A viewing platform and interpretive signage help visitors to see and identify waterfowl from migrating swans and scoters to breeding birds such as teal, grebes, mallard and gulls. Shorebirds such as plovers, sandpipers, avocet and snipe are also common. The brush and cattails surrounding the slough harbour marsh wren, blackbirds and sparrows.

Pine Lake

Access: Highway 2 south for 16 kilometres, then east on Highway 42 for 20 kilometres to reach the north end of Pine Lake; Highway 816 takes you to the south end of the lake

Pine Lake is a nine kilometre-long lake edged by sandy beaches and spruce forests. Several resorts with camping facilities and cabins, picnic areas and boat launches, cater to visitors staying for an afternoon or longer. Grocery stores, laundromats, a service station and many recreational opportunities are all handy.

The lake was known as Devil's Pine or Ghostpine Lake by native people since a massacre in the early 1800s. One Cree warrior returned from a hunting trip to find his whole tribe killed during the night. Painting his face black, he set out to avenge the slaughter. The warrior would raid the enemy's camp at night or ambush stragglers, terrorizing the enemy until they fled the lake and the avenging 'ghost'.

Any information centre can help you contact one of the resorts for further information and reservations.

Anthony Henday Museum

Access: Main street in Delburne
Contact: 403-749-2436
Open: Seasonally

The Anthony Henday Museum is housed in Delburne's historic train station next to the water tower. Exhibits highlight the farming, coal mining and railway industries of the area, education, local businesses and home life of the past.

A treed campground and playground are right across the street. The museum also serves as a tourist information centre.

Alberta Prairie Steam Tours

Access: Stettler
Contact: 1–800–282–3994 or 403-742-2811
Open: Seasonally

Step onto a steam–powered train for an entertaining trip to places like Big Valley, Rowley, Donalda, Meeting Creek and Coronation. Each stop has something interesting to offer, from restored train stations to local festivals, breathtaking badlands to an unrivalled lamp collection. There are also special theme tours, murder mysteries and musical performers on board and train hold–ups.

St. Ann Ranch
Access: From Highway 21 enter Trochu; the St. Ann Ranch is at the southeast end of the town
Contact: 403-442–3924
Open: Year-round; the tea room operates seasonally.
The St. Ann Ranch is a provincially designated historic site. The ranch is one of several established in the Trochu area by French cavalry officers. Most returned to France at the beginning of World War I. The St. Ann is owned by the descendants of one of these officers.

Visitors to the ranch have the opportunity to take part in afternoon tea in the ranch house, now a popular tea room and bed and breakfast. Several outbuildings, including a 1904 log cabin and 1907 post office, are on the grounds. Visitors can also see historic photographs, antiques and artifacts from the French Sisters of Charity of Our Lady of Evron dating to 1909.

Trochu Valley Historical Museum
Access: Arena Avenue in Trochu
Contact: 403-442–3935 or 403-442–3916
Open: Seasonally
Trochu's history is exhibited in this museum and archives. Look for native artifacts, pioneer home items, dinosaur fossils and a good collection of artifacts from St. Mary's Hospital, founded in 1909 by three sisters from the order of the Sisters of Charity of Our Lady of Evron from France.

Arboretum at Trochu
Access: Highway 21 south to Trochu, turn east at the cemetery on North Road at the north end of town (visible from highway)
Contact: 403-442–2111
Open: Seasonally
The Arboretum is a showcase of trees, shrubs and seasonal plantings. Over 1,000 trees and shrubs, planted between 1920 and the 1950s, were brought here from around the world by the previous owners. The walkways are wheelchair accessible and many benches are placed throughout the site to allow you to rest and enjoy the surroundings.

For More Information

A wealth of information on the natural and cultural history of Central Alberta is available for the asking. Listed below are some of the main facilities and organizations you may wish to contact.

City Facilities

Waskasoo Park – City of Red Deer
Box 5008
Red Deer, Alberta
T4N 3T4
General Information: 403-342–8159
Bower Ponds Pavilion: 403-347–9777
Fort Normandeau: 403-347–7550
Heritage Ranch (Trail Rides): 403-347–4977
Lions Campground: 403-342–8183
Picnic Shelter Reservations: 403-342–6100
River Bend Golf Course and Recreation Area: 403-343–8311
– information on trails, Waskasoo Park, picnic shelter bookings

Kerry Wood Nature Centre
6300 – 45 Avenue
Red Deer, Alberta
T4N 3M4
Tel. 403-346–2010

Red Deer and District Museum
Box 800
Red Deer, Alberta
T4N 5H2
Tel. 403-343–6844

Red Deer and District Archives
Box 800
Red Deer, Alberta
T4N 5H2
Tel. 403-343–6842

Red Deer Visitor and Convention Bureau
Visitor Information Centre, Heritage Ranch
Box 5008
Red Deer, Alberta
T4N 3T4
Tel. 403-346–0180 1-800-215-8946
– information on attractions and events in and around Red Deer

Local Organizations

Kerry Wood Nature Centre Association
Box 1199
Red Deer, Alberta
T4N 6S6
Tel. 403-346–2010
– a co–operating association for the Kerry Wood Nature Centre; operates
the bookstore, engages in special programming and fundraising

Red Deer and District Museum Society
Box 800
Red Deer, Alberta
T4N 5H2
Tel. 403-343–6844
– this organization supports the museum with volunteers and
fundraising

Red Deer River Naturalists Society
Box 785
Red Deer, Alberta
T4N 5H2
Tel. 403-347–8200
– host monthly meetings at Kerry Wood Nature Centre the fourth
Thursday of the month, except for May through September; field trips
during the summer; environmental advocacy group

Red Deer Fish and Game Association
Box 2
Red Deer, Alberta
T4N 5E8
– committed to sportsmanship, proper hunting practices,
conservation of wildlife and habitat

Ellis Bird Farm Ltd.
Box 2980
Lacombe, Alberta
T0C 1S0
Tel. 403-346–2211
– established to conserve cavity nesting birds, especially mountain bluebirds, education and research programs

Provincial and Federal Organizations and Government Departments

Federation of Alberta Naturalists
Box 1472
Edmonton, Alberta
T5J 2H5
Tel. 403-453–8629
– provincial association of naturalist clubs, quarterly magazine, compilation of annual species counts

Archaeological Society of Alberta
1202 Lansdowne Avenue SW
Calgary, Alberta
T2S 1A6
Tel. 403-243–4340
– members meet in different areas of the province to discuss Alberta archaeology; speakers, workshops

Historical Society of Alberta
325 – 8 Avenue SW
Calgary, Alberta
T2P 1C2
Tel. 403-261–3662
– provincial association of history societies

Alberta Agriculture
#101, 4920 – 51 Street
Red Deer, Alberta
T4N 6K8
Tel. 403-340–5364
– information on agriculture, farmer's markets, market gardens

Alberta Environmental Protection, Fish and Wildlife Division
4911 – 51 Street
Red Deer, Alberta
T4N 6V4
Tel. 403-340–5142
– hunting and fishing permits and regulations, wildlife conservation and research, population studies, education programs (Project Wild, Watchable Wildlife)

Alberta Environmental Protection, Land Management Branch
Natural and Protected Areas Section
4th Floor, Petroleum Plaza South
9915 – 108 Street
Edmonton, Alberta
T5K 2C9
Tel. 403-427–5209
– information on natural areas in Alberta, becoming a volunteer steward

Environment Canada, Canadian Wildlife Service
2nd Floor, 4999 – 98 Avenue
Edmonton, Alberta
T6B 2X3
Tel. 403-468–8919
– wildlife conservation and research, endangered wildlife

Ducks Unlimited
#8, 5580 – 45 Street
Red Deer, Alberta
T4N 1L1
Tel. 403-342–1314
– conservation of waterfowl and wetlands for hunting

Canadian Nature Federation
Suite 520, 1 Nicholas Street
Ottawa, Ontario
K1N 7B7
Tel: 613–562–3447
– national organization representing Canadian naturalists, naturalist clubs and provincial federations, and promoting conservation education and environmental preservation

Canadian Wildlife Federation
2740 Queensview Drive
Ottawa, Ontario
K2B 1A2
– umbrella organization for fish and game associations; conservation of wildlife

Nature Conservancy of Canada
707 – 8 Avenue SW
Calgary, Alberta
T2P 3V3
Tel. 403-294-7064
– land conservation for preservation of species

Trans–Canada Trail Foundation
6104 Sherbrooke West
Montreal, PQ
H4A 1Y3
Tel. 1–800–465–3636
– organization trying to set up a cross–Canada trail system

Heritage Canada
P.O. Box 1358, Stn B
Ottawa, Ontario
K1P 5R4
Tel: 613–237–1066

Alberta Museums Association
Rossdale House
9829 – 103 Street
Edmonton, Alberta
T5J 0X9
Tel: 403-424–2626
– semi–professional organization representing museums in Alberta

Alberta Historical Resources Foundation
Old St. Stephen's College
8820 – 112 Street
Edmonton, Alberta
T6G 2P8
Tel: 403-431–2300
– foundation supporting heritage sites, buildings and related projects

Amphibians and Reptiles of Waskasoo Park

Common Name	Latin Name	Habitat Preference
Amphibians		
❏ Tiger salamander	*Ambystoma tigrinum*	W, Md
❏ Chorus frog	*Pseudacris triseriata*	W, Ow
❏ Wood frog	*Rana sylvatica*	W, Ow
❏ Leopard frog	*R. pipiens*	W, Ow
❏ Dakota toad	*Bufo hemiophrys*	P, M, W
Reptiles		
❏ Red–sided garter snake	*Thamnophis sirtalis parietalis*	W, Md, P
❏ Wandering garter snake	*T. elegans vagrans*	Md
❏ Plains garter snake	*T. radix*	W, Md, P

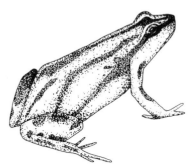

Legend

S = spruce	OW = open water
P = poplar	D = disturbed
M = mixed woods	Sh = shrub
C = cattail	Md = meadow
	W = wet meadow

Fishes of the Red Deer River
& Surrounding Lakes — Near the City of Red Deer

Common Name & Order	Latin Name

Acipenseriformes
Sturgeon family
❏ Lake sturgeon   *Acipenser fulvescens*

Osteoglossiformes
Mooneye family
❏ Goldeye   *Hiodon alosoides*
❏ Mooneye   *H. tergisus*

Cypriniformes
Minnow family
❏ Lake chub   *Couesius plumbeus*
❏ Fathead minnow   *Pimephales promelas*
❏ Spottail shiner   *Notropis hudsonius*
❏ Longnose dace   *Rhinichthys cataractae*

Sucker family
❏ Longnose sucker   *Catostomus catostomus*
❏ White sucker   *C. commersoni*
❏ Mountain sucker   *C. platyrhynchus*
❏ Northern (or Shorthead)   *Moxostoma macrolepidotum*
   redhorse

Salmoniformes
Pike family
❏ Northern pike   *Esox lucius*

Trout family
❏ Lake whitefish   *Coregonus clupeaformis*
❏ Mountain whitefish   *Prosopium williamsoni*
❏ Cutthroat trout   *Salmo clarki*—upstream of dam
❏ Rainbow trout   *S. gairdneri*—upstream of dam
❏ Brown trout   *S. trutta*—near mouth of Blindman River
❏ Bull trout   *Salvelinus confluentus*
❏ Dolly Varden   *S. malma*—upstream of dam
❏ Brook trout   *S. fontinalis*—upstream of dam

Percopsiformes
Trout–Perch family
❑ Trout–perch   *Percopsis omiscomaycus*

Gadiformes
Cod family
❑ Burbot("ling cod")   *Lota lota*

Gasterosteiformes
Stickleback family
❑ Brook stickleback   *Culaea inconstans*

Scorpaeniformes
Sculpin family
❑ Spoonhead sculpin   *Cottus ricei*

Perciformes
Perch family
❑ Iowa Darter   *Etheostoma exile*
❑ Yellow Perch   *Perca flavescens*
❑ Sauger   *Stizostedion canadense*
❑ Walleye   *S. vitreum vitreum*

Birds of Waskasoo Park

Common Name	Latin Name	*Habitat Preference and Order
Gaviiformes		
❏ Common loon	*Gavia immer*	OW
Podicipediformes		
❏ Red–necked grebe	*Podiceps grisegena*	OW, C
❏ Eared grebe	*P. nigricollis*	OW, C
❏ Horned grebe	*P. auritus*	OW, C
❏ Pied–billed grebe	*Podilymbus podiceps*	OW, C
Ciconiiformes		
❏ Great blue heron	*Ardea herodias*	OW, C
❏ American bittern	*Botaurus lentiginosus*	OW, C
❏ Sandhill crane	*Grus canadensis*	Md
Anseriformes		
❏ Canada goose	*Branta canadensis*	OW, W, Md
❏ Mallard	*Anas platyrhinchos*	OW, C, Sh, W
❏ Gadwall	*A. strepera*	OW, C, Sh, W
❏ Pintail	*A. acuta*	OW, C, Sh, W
❏ Green–winged teal	*A. crecca*	OW, C, Sh, W
❏ Blue–winged teal	*A. discors*	OW, C, Sh, W
❏ American wigeon	*A. americana*	OW, C, Sh, W
❏ Northern shoveler	*A. clypeata*	OW, C, Sh, W
❏ Redhead	*Aythya americana*	OW, C, Sh
❏ Ring–necked duck	*Ay. collaris*	OW, C, Sh
❏ Canvasback	*Ay. valisineria*	OW, C, Sh, W
❏ Lesser scaup	*Ay. affinis*	OW, C, Sh, W
❏ Common goldeneye	*Bucephala clangula*	OW, Sh, S, M, P
❏ Bufflehead	*B. albeola*	OW, Sh, S, M, P
❏ White–winged scoter	*Melanitta fusca*	OW, Sh
❏ Ruddy duck	*Oxyura jamaicensis*	OW, C
❏ Red–breasted merganser	*Mergus serrator*	OW
❏ Common merganser	*M. merganser*	OW
Falconiformes		
❏ Northern goshawk	*Accipiter gentilis*	S, M
❏ Cooper's hawk	*A. cooperii*	M, P
❏ Sharp–shinned hawk	*A. striatus*	S, M

❏ Rough–legged hawk	*Buteo lagopus*	Md, P, M
❏ Red–tailed hawk	*B. jamaicensis*	most
❏ Broad–winged hawk	*B. platypterus*	M, P, Md
❏ Swainson's hawk	*B. swainsoni*	most
❏ Northern harrier	*Circus cyaneus*	W, Md
❏ Bald eagle	*Haliaeetus leucocephalus*	OW (winter)
❏ Osprey	*Pandion haliaetus*	OW
❏ Gyrfalcon	*Falco rusticolus*	Md, Sh (winter)
❏ Peregrine falcon	*Falco peregrinus*	S, P, M
❏ Merlin	*Falco columbarius*	most
❏ American kestrel	*F. sparverius*	most

Galliformes

❏ Ruffed grouse	*Bonasa umbellus*	Sh, Md, P
❏ Spruce grouse	*Dendragapus canadensis*	M, P
❏ Sharp–tailed grouse	*Tympanuchus phasianellus*	Md
❏ Ring–necked pheasant	*Phasianus colchicus*	Md, Sh, P
❏ Gray partridge	*Perdix perdix*	Sh, Md

Gruiformes

❏ Virginia rail	*Rallus limicola*	OW, C
❏ Sora	*Porzana carolina*	OW, C
❏ American coot	*Fulica americana*	OW, C

Charadriiformes

❏ Killdeer	*Charadrius vociferus*	OW, W
❏ American avocet	*Recurvirostra americana*	OW, W
❏ Greater yellowlegs	*Tringa melanoleuca*	OW, W, Md, Sh, P
❏ Solitary sandpiper	*T. solitaria*	OW, W, S, M, P
❏ Spotted sandpiper	*Actitis macularia*	OW, W
❏ Common snipe	*Gallinago gallinago*	OW, W
❏ Wilson's phalarope	*Phalaropus tricolor*	OW, W
❏ California gull	*Larus californicus*	OW
❏ Ring–billed gull	*L. delawarensis*	OW, W, Md
❏ Franklin's gull	*L. pipixcan*	OW
❏ Bonaparte's gull	*L. philadelphia*	OW
❏ Common tern	*Sterna hirundo*	OW
❏ Black tern	*Chlidonias niger*	OW

Columbiformes

❏ Mourning dove	*Zenaida macroura*	P, M, Md, D
❏ Rock dove	*Columba livia*	most

Strigiformes

❑ Great horned owl	*Bubo virginianus*	M, P, Md
❑ Long–eared owl	*Asio otus*	Md
❑ Short–eared owl	*A. flammeus*	Md
❑ Snowy owl (winter)	*Nyctea scandiaca*	Md, Sh
❑ Barred owl	*Strix varia*	S, M
❑ Hawk owl (winter)	*Surnia ulula*	Md, Sh, P
❑ Boreal owl (winter)	*Aegolius funereus*	S
❑ Saw–whet owl	*A. acadicus*	S, M, P

Caprimulgiformes

❑ Common nighthawk	*Chordeiles minor*	most

Apodiformes

❑ Ruby–throated hummingbird	*Archilochus colubris*	Md

Coraciiformes

❑ Belted kingfisher	*Ceryle alcyon*	OW

Piciformes

❑ Yellow–bellied sapsucker	*Sphyrapicus varius*	M, P
❑ Downy woodpecker	*Picoides pubescens*	M, P
❑ Hairy woodpecker	*P. villosus*	M, P
❑ Three–toed woodpecker	*P. tridactylus*	S, M, P
❑ Black–backed woodpecker	*Picoides arcticus*	S, M, P
❑ Northern flicker	*Colaptes auratus*	P, Md
❑ Pileated woodpecker	*Dryocopus pileatus*	M, P

Passeriformes

❑ Western wood peewee	*Contopus sordidulus*	S, M, P
❑ Traill's flycatcher	*Empidonax traillii*	Sh
❑ Least flycatcher	*Empidonax minimus*	P, M
❑ Eastern phoebe	*Sayornis phoebe*	OW, Sh, D
❑ Say's phoebe	*Sayornis saya*	Sh, Md
❑ Eastern kingbird	*Tyrannus tyrannus*	P, Md
❑ Purple martin	*Progne subis*	most
❑ Tree swallow	*Tachycineta bicolor*	most
❑ Cliff swallow	*Hirundo pyrrhonta*	most
❑ Bank swallow	*Riparia riparia*	most
❑ Northern rough–winged swallow	*Stelgidopteryx serripennis*	most
❑ Barn swallow	*Hirundo rustica*	most
❑ Blue jay	*Cyanocitta cristata*	most

❑ Steller's jay	*C. stelleri*	S (winter)
❑ Gray jay	*Perisoreus canadensis*	S (winter)
❑ Black–billed magpie	*Pica pica*	most
❑ Common raven	*Corvus corax*	S (winter)
❑ American crow	*C. brachyrhynchos*	most
❑ Black–capped chickadee	*Parus atricapillus*	S, M
❑ Boreal chickadee	*P. hudsonicus*	S, M
❑ Red–breasted nuthatch	*Sitta canadensis*	S, M
❑ White–breasted nuthatch	*S. carolinensis*	S, M
❑ Brown creeper	*Certhia americana*	S
❑ House wren	*Troglodytes aedon*	P, Sh
❑ Marsh wren	*Cistothorus palustris*	C
❑ Golden–crowned kinglet	*Regulus satrapa*	S (winter)
❑ Ruby–crowned kinglet	*R. calendula*	S, M
❑ Mountain bluebird	*Sialia currocoides*	Md
❑ Veery	*Catharus fuscescens*	P, Sh
❑ American robin	*Turdus migratorius*	M, P, Md
❑ Gray catbird	*Dumetella carolinensis*	Sh
❑ Brown thrasher	*Toxostoma rufum*	Sh
❑ Sprague's pipit	*Anthus spragueii*	Md
❑ Cedar waxwing	*Bombycilla cedrorum*	most
❑ Bohemian waxwing	*B. garrulus*	most
❑ Northern shrike	*Lanius excubitor*	Md, Sh, P, M (w)
❑ Loggerhead shrike	*L. ludovicianus*	Sh
❑ European starling	*Sturnus vulgaris*	most
❑ Solitary vireo	*Vireo solitarius*	M, P
❑ Warbling vireo	*V. gilvus*	P
❑ Philadelphia vireo	*V. philadelphicus*	M, P
❑ Red–eyed vireo	*V. olivaceus*	P, Sh
❑ Tennessee warbler	*Vermivora peregrina*	Sh, M
❑ Orange–crowned warbler	*V. celata*	Sh, M, P
❑ Yellow warbler	*Dendroica petechia*	Sh
❑ Yellow–rumped warbler	*D. coronata*	Sh
❑ Blackpoll warbler (?)	*D. striata*	Sh
❑ Black and white warbler	*Mniotilta varia*	Sh, M
❑ Common yellowthroat	*Geothlypis trichas*	W, Sh
❑ Western tanager	*Piranga ludoviciana*	S, M
❑ Rose–breasted grosbeak	*Pheucticus ludovicianus*	Sh, M, P
❑ Evening grosbeak	*Coccothraustes vespertinus*	M, S
❑ Pine grosbeak	*Pinicola enucleator*	S, M, P
❑ Chipping sparrow	*Spizella passerina*	Sh, M, P
❑ Clay–coloured sparrow	*S. pallida*	Sh, Md
❑ Vesper sparrow	*Pooecetes gramineus*	Md

❏ Savannah sparrow	*Passerculus sandwichensis*	Md, W
❏ Baird's sparrow	*Ammodramus bairdii*	Md, Sh
❏ LeConte's sparrow	*A. leconteii*	Sh, W
❏ Sharp–tailed sparrow	*A. caudacutus*	W, Sh, Md
❏ Song sparrow	*Melospiza melodia*	Sh
❏ Lincoln's sparrow	*M. lincolnii*	Sh
❏ White–throated sparrow	*Zonotrichia albicollis*	Sh, S, M
❏ White–crowned sparrow	*Z. leucophrys*	Sh, P
❏ Dark–eyed junco	*Junco hyemalis*	M, S
❏ Snow bunting	*Plectrophenax nivalis*	migrant
❏ Red–winged blackbird	*Agelaius phoeniceus*	OW, C, Sh
❏ Western meadowlark	*Sturnella neglecta*	Md
❏ Yellow–headed blackbird	*Xanthocephalus xanthocephalus*	OW, C
❏ Rusty blackbird	*Euphagus carolinus*	Sh
❏ Brewer's blackbird	*E. cyanocephalus*	Sh
❏ Common grackle	*Quiscalus quiscula*	M, Sh
❏ Brown–headed cowbird	*Molothrus ater*	Md
❏ Northern oriole	*Icterus galbula*	P
❏ Purple finch	*Carpodacus purpureus*	M, P
❏ Red crossbill	*Loxia curvirostra*	S
❏ White–winged crossbill	*L. leucoptera*	S
❏ Common redpoll	*Carduelis flammea*	Md, M, P, Sh
❏ Hoary redpoll	*C. hornemanni*	Md, M, P, Sh
❏ Pine siskin	*C. pinus*	S, M, Md, D
❏ American goldfinch	*C. tristis*	Sh, Md
❏ House sparrow	*Passer domesticus*	most

Flowering Plants of Waskasoo Park

Pinaceae

❑ *Larix laricina* — tamarack
❑ *Picea glauca* — white spruce
❑ *P. mariana* — black spruce

Equisetaceae

❑ *Equisetum arvense* — common horsetail

Typhaceae

❑ *Typha latifolia* — cattail

Alismaceae

❑ *Alisma plantago–aquatica* — common water plantain
❑ *Sagittaria cuneata* — arrowhead

Juncaceae

❑ *Juncus sp.* — rushes

Lemnaceae

❑ *Lemna sp.* — duckweed
❑ *Spirodela polyrhiza* — larger duckweed

Liliaceae

❑ *Allium cernuum* — nodding onion
❑ *A. textile* — prairie onion
❑ *Disporum trachycarpum* — fairybells
❑ *Lilium philadelphicum* — western wood lily
❑ *Maianthemum canadense* — wild lily of the valley
❑ *Smilacina stellata* — star–flowered solomon's seal
❑ *Zygadenus elegans* — smooth camas

Iridaceae

❑ *Sisyrinchium montanum* — blue–eyed grass

Orchidaceae

❑ *Cypripedium calceolus* — large yellow ladyslipper
❑ *Orchis rotundifolia* — round-leaved orchid
❑ *Spiranthes romanzoffiana* — hooded lady's tresses

Salicaceae

❏ *Populus balsamifera*   balsam poplar
❏ *P. tremuloides*   trembling aspen
❏ *Salix sp.*   willow (various species)

Betulaceae

❏ *Alnus tenuifolia*   alder
❏ *Betula papyrifera*   paper birch
❏ *B. glandulifera*   swamp birch
❏ *Corylus cornuta*   beaked hazelnut

Urticaceae

❏ *Urtica dioica*   stinging nettle

Santalaceae

❏ *Comandra pallida*   pale comandra
❏ *Geocaulon umbellata*   bastard toadflax

Chenopodiaceae

❏ *Chenopodium capitatum*   strawberry blite
❏ *Salsola kali*   Russian–thistle

Caryophyllaceae

❏ *Cerastium sp.*   chickweed
❏ *Stellaria sp.*

Ranunculaceae

❏ *Clematis verticellaris*   purple clematis
❏ *Actaea rubra*   baneberry
❏ *Anemone patens*   prairie crocus
❏ *A. multifida*   cut–leaved anemone
❏ *A. canadensis*   Canada anemone
❏ *Aquilegia brevistyla*   small flowered columbine
❏ *Ranunculus subrigidus*   white watercrowfoot
❏ *Thalictrum venulosum*   veiny meadow rue
❏ *Calthus palustris*   marsh marigold

Fumariaceae

❏ *Corydalis aurea*   golden corydalis

Cruciferae

❏ *Thlapsi arvense*   stinkweed

Saxifragaceae
❏ *Mitella nuda* — bishop's cap
❏ *Ribes oxyancanthoides* — wild gooseberry
❏ *R. triste* — wild red currant
❏ *R. americanum* — wild black currant

Rosaceae
❏ *Amelanchier alnifolia* — saskatoon
❏ *Fragaria virginiana* — wild strawberry
❏ *Geum triflorum* — three–flowered avens
❏ *Potentilla fruticosa* — shrubby cinquefoil
❏ *P. anserina* — silverweed
❏ *P. norvegica* — rough cinquefoil
❏ *Prunus virginiana* — red chokecherry
❏ *P. pensylvanica* — pin cherry
❏ *Rosa acicularis* — prickly rose
❏ *Rubus idaeus* — wild red raspberry
❏ *R. pubescens* — dewberry
❏ *Sorbus aucuparia* — mountain ash

Leguminosae
❏ *Hedysarum alpinum* — hedysarum
❏ *Lathyrus ochroleucus* cream coloured vetchling
❏ *Medicago sativa* — alfalfa
❏ *M. lupulina* — black medick
❏ *Melilotus alba* white sweet clover
❏ *M. officinalis* — yellow sweet clover
❏ *Oxytropis sp.* — locoweed
❏ *Thermopsis rhombifolia* — goldenbean
❏ *Trifolium pratense* — red clover
❏ *Vicia americana* — wild vetch

Geraniaceae
❏ *Geranium richardsonii* — wild white geranium

Polygalaceae
❏ *Polygala senega* — Seneca root

Violaceae
❏ *Viola adunca* — early blue violet
❏ *V. rugulosa* — western Canada violet
❏ *V. renifolia* — kidney–leaved violet

Elaeagnaceae
❏ *Elaeagnus commutata*   wolf willow
❏ *Shepherdia canadensis*   buffaloberry

Onagraceae
❏ *Epilobium angustifolium*   fireweed

Araliaceae
❏ *Aralia nudicaulis*   wild sarsaparilla

Haloragaceae
❏ *Hippuris vulgaris*   mare's tail

Umbelliferae
❏ *Cicuta maculata*   water–hemlock
❏ *Heracleum lanatum*   cow parsnip
❏ *Osmorhiza aristata*   sweet Cicely
❏ *Sanicula marilandica*   snakeroot
❏ *Zizia aptera*   heart–leaved alexander

Cornaceae
❏ *Cornus canadensis*   bunchberry
❏ *C. stolonifera*   red–osier dogwood

Pyrolaceae
❏ *Moneses uniflora*   one–flowered wintergreen
❏ *Pyrola asarifolia*   pink wintergreen
❏ *P. secunda*   one–sided wintergreen

Ericaceae
❏ *Arctostaphylos uva–ursi*   bearberry

Primulaceae
❏ *Dodecathon pauciflorum*   shooting star
❏ *Lysimachia ciliata*   fringed loosestrife

Apocynaceae
❏ *Apocynum androsaemifolium* spreading dogbane

Boraginaceae
❏ *Mertensia paniculata*   lungwort

Labiatae
❏ *Agastache foeniculum*   giant hyssop
❏ *Galeopsis tetrahit*   hempnettle
❏ *Mentha arvensis*   wild mint

❑ *Scutellaria galericulata*   marsh skullcap
❑ *Stachys palustris*   marsh hedge nettle

Solanaceae
❑ *Hyoscyamus niger*   black henbane

Scrophulariaceae
❑ *Castilleja sp.*   Indian paintbrush

Rubiaceae
❑ *Galium boreale*   northern bedstraw
❑ *G. triflorum*   sweet–scented bedstraw

Caprifoliaceae
❑ *Lonicera dioca*   twining honeysuckle
❑ *L. involucrata*   bracted honeysuckle
❑ *Sambucus racemosa*   red elderberry
❑ *Symphoricarpos albus*   snowberry
❑ *S. occidentalis*   buckbrush
❑ *Viburnum edule*   low–bush cranberry
❑ *V. opulus*   high–bush cranberry
❑ *Linnaea borealis*   twinflower

Campanulaceae
❑ *Campanula rotundifolia*   harebell

Compositae
❑ *Crepis tectorum*   narrow–leaved hawksbeard
❑ *Taraxacum officinale*   dandelion
❑ *Tragopogon dubius*   goatsbeard
❑ *Achillea millefolium*   yarrow
❑ *Antennaria sp.*   pussytoes
❑ *Artemesia firgida*   pasture sage
❑ *Cirsium sp.*   thistle
❑ *Erigeron philadelphicus*   Philadelphia fleabane
❑ *Erigeron sp.*   fleabane
❑ *Gaillardia aristata*   gaillardia
❑ *Matricaria matricarioides*   wild chamomile
❑ *Petasites sagittus*   arrow–leaved coltsfoot
❑ *P. palmatus*   palmate–leaved coltsfoot
❑ *Senecio vulgaris*   common groundsel
❑ *Solidago sp.*   goldenrod
❑ *Aster pansus*   many flowered aster

Mosses & Lichens

Latin Name	Common name, if available, and habitat

Mosses

❑ *Pylaisia polyantha* — aspen stocking moss; on aspen poplar
❑ *Brachythecium salebrosum* — branched, prostrate
❑ *Minium cuspidatum* — leaflike
❑ *Aulacomnium palustre* — moist ground, tomentose
❑ *Ceratodon purpureus* — on soil; carpets; hooked capsule, unbranched
❑ *Dicranum sp.* — on logs; capsule not hooked and at right angle or straight
❑ *Pohlia nutans* — on rotten logs; has big leaves
❑ *Orthotrichum sp.* — in fissures of balsam poplar; pincushion or upright and unbranched leaves
❑ *Hypnum cupressiforme* — feather–like moss; sickle–shaped leaves
❑ *Ptilium crista–castrensis* — flat; like Christmas tree
❑ *Pleurozium shreberi* — reddish stem; not as flat
❑ *Drepanocladus aduncus* — in sloughs with basic pH
❑ *Eurhyncium pulchellum* — blunt tipped leaves
❑ *Abietinella abietina* — feather–like moss; wiry

Lichens

❑ *Lecanora sp.*
❑ *Bacidia sphaeroides*
❑ *Lecidea sp.*
❑ *Candelariella aurella*
❑ *Calicium sp.*
❑ *Parmelia albertana*
❑ *P. sulcata*
❑ *P. flaventior*
❑ *Cetraria halei*
❑ *Physcia stellaris*
❑ *P. orbicularis*
❑ *P. adscendens*
❑ *Hypogymnia physodes*
❑ *Peltigera canina*
❑ *Xanthoria fallax*
❑ *Cladonia sp.*
❑ *Usnea sp.*
❑ *Ramalina sp.*
❑ *Evernia mesomorpha*

Mammals of Waskasoo Park

Common Name and Order	Latin Name	Habitat Preference
Insectivores		
❏ Masked shrew	*Sorex cinereus*	S, W, Md, P
❏ Arctic shrew	*Sorex arcticus*	W, Sh
❏ Water shrew	*Sorex palustris*	marginal
❏ Pygmy shrew	*Microsorex hoyi*	G, M, Md
Bats		
❏ Little brown bat	*Myotis lucifugus*	S, M, P
❏ Silver–haired bat	*Lasionycteris noctivagans*	S, M, P, OW
❏ Pale big brown bat	*Eptesicus fuscus*	most
❏ Hoary bat	*Lasiurus cinereus*	S, M
Hares & Rabbits		
❏ Nuttall's cottontail	*Sylvilagus nutallii*	Sh, Md
❏ White–tailed jack rabbit	*Lepus townsendii*	Md
❏ Varying hare	*L. americanus*	S, M
Rodents		
❏ Thirteen–lined ground squirrel	*Spermophilus tridecemlineatus*	P, Sh
❏ Richardson's ground squirrel	*S. richardsonii*	Md
❏ Franklin ground squirrel	*S. franklinii*	P, M
❏ Least chipmunk	*Eutamias minimus*	S, M
❏ Red squirrel	*Tamiasciurus hudsonicus*	S, M
❏ Flying squirrel	*Glaucomys sabrinus*	S
❏ Northern pocket gopher	*Thomomys talpoides*	Md, W
❏ Beaver	*Castor canadensis*	OW, P, Sh
❏ Deer mouse	*Peromyscus maniculatis*	most
❏ Red–backed vole	*Cleithrionomys gapperi*	S, M
❏ Heather vole	*Phenacomys intermedius*	S
❏ Meadow vole	*Microtus pennsylvanicus*	W, Md
❏ Muskrat	*Ondatra zibethicus*	OW, S
❏ Jumping mouse	*Zapus princeps*	W, Sh
❏ Porcupine	*Erethizon dorsatum*	S, M, P, Sh

Carnivores

❑ Coyote	*Canis latrans*	most
❑ Fox	*Vulpes vulpes*	P, Sh, P, Md
❑ Ermine	*Mustela erminea*	S, M
❑ Least weasel	*M. rixos*	most
❑ Long–tailed weasel	*M. frenata*	Md
❑ Mink	*M. vison*	OW, Sh, W
❑ Badger	*Taxidea taxus*	Md
❑ Striped skunk	*Mephitus mephitus*	most

Ungulates

❑ Mule deer	*Odocoileus hemonius*	Sh, P, Md
❑ White–tailed deer	*O. virginianus*	Sh, P, Md
❑ Moose	*Alces alces*	S, W, Sh, C, Md

Further Reading

Dawe, Michael J. *Red Deer, An Illustrated History*, Burlington, Windsor Publishing, 1989

Dawe, Wellington B. *History of Red Deer*, Red Deer, Kiwanis Club, 1967 (out of print but available at public library)

Helgason, Gail *The First Albertans*, Edmonton, Lone Pine Publishing, 1987

MacGregor, J. G. *A History of Alberta*, Edmonton, Hurtig Publishing, 1972
  Father Lacombe, Edmonton, Hurtig Publishers, 1975

Meeres, E. L. *The Homesteads That Nurtured a City*, Red Deer, Fletcher Printing, 2nd edition, no date

North Red Deer 75 Anniversary Committee *The Little Village That Grew*, Red Deer, Adviser Graphics, 1987

Parker, Georgean C. *Proud Beginnings: A Pictorial History of Red Deer*, Red Deer, Red Deer and District Museum Society, 1981

Ross, Jane and Dan Kyba *David Thompson Highway: A Hiking Guide*, Rocky Mountain Books, 1995

Wood, Kerry *A Corner of Canada*, Calgary, John D. McAra Ltd., 1967
  The Sanctuary, Edmonton, Hamly Press, 1952
  Red Deer, A Love Story, Red Deer, Adviser Printers, 1975
  Maskepetoon—The Great Chief, Toronto, MacMillan of Canada, 1960
  Mickey the Beaver and Other Stories, MacMillan of Canada, 1964, reprinted 1994 by Red Deer & District Museum Society and Kerry Wood Nature Centre Association

Smith, Harvey J. Kerry Wood Nature Centre Association Natural History Series, Red Deer, Kerry Wood Nature Centre Association, 1990

The Gaetz Lakes Sanctuary
The Amphibians and Reptiles of Waskasoo Park
The Fishes of the Red Deer River
The Forest Birds of Waskasoo Park
The Water Birds of Waskasoo Park
The Grassland Birds of Waskasoo Park
The Trees and Shrubs of Waskasoo Park
The Grassland Wildflowers of Waskasoo Park
The Woodland Wildflowers of Waskasoo Park

During the planning of Waskasoo Park, several background documents on the natural and cultural features of the park area were produced. These reports are available at the Red Deer and District Archives.

Index

Also by Anna Robertson

A Guide to Fish Creek Provincial Park

A natural history guide to Canada's largest urban park, Fish Creek Park's forests and meadows harbour an incredible variety of plants and wildlife, which are described in the first half of the book together with easy-to-understand information on how the valley was formed and what evidence has been left behind by the first visitors 8,000 years ago.

Beautifully illustrated with drawings throughout by wildlife artist Gary Ross.

128 pages, photos $12.95

A hiking guide from Rocky Mountain Books

David Thompson Highway: A Hiking Guide
Jane Ross & Daniel Kyba

Alberta's David Thompson Highway passes through breathtaking mountain scenery between Nordegg and Banff National Park.

All 69 hikes start from the highway and range from walks of one or two hours to three-day backpacks. The authors, who spent two summers hiking all the trails, use sidebars and feature boxes to highlight the area's place names, history, geology and flora.

256 pages, 146 b&w photos, maps $16.95

Order Form

❏ Exploring Red Deer's Waskasoo Park   ___ x $14.95 _____

❏ David Thompson Hwy. Hiking Guide   ___ x $16.95 _____

❏ Fish Creek Provincial Park   ___ x $12.95 _____

Total for books _____

7% GST _____

Postage $3 for 1st book plus 50¢ each additional book   _____

Total amount _____

Paying by ❏ **Cheque**   ❏ **Visa** (sorry, we do not accept other credit cards)

Visa number ....

Expiry Date ....

Signed ....

Name ....

Address ....

....

City .... Postal Code ....

Tel: ....

Mail or fax to:
Rocky Mountain Books
#4 Spruce Centre SW
Calgary, Alberta T3C 3B3
Fax: 403-249-2968
Tel: 403-249-9490

Use our 800 number to order by telephone **1-800-566-3336**